The Book of Emet

The TRUE Story of Jesus

by Rabbi Martin K. Vesole

Copyright © 2014, 2021 by Rabbi Martin K. Vesole

This book is licensed for your personal enjoyment only and may not be re-sold or given away to other people. If you would like to share this book with another person, please purchase an additional copy for each recipient. Thank you for respecting the hard work of this author.

All rights reserved. No part of this book may be reproduced or transmitted in any manner whatsoever without written permission, except in the case of brief quotations embodied in critical articles or reviews. Please do not participate in or encourage the piracy of copyrighted materials in violation of the author's rights. Purchase only authorized editions.

Published by Shalom Rav Publications

ISBN 978-1-937416-03-4

Library of Congress Control No. 2014915497

Contents

	Foreword 1
Chapter 1	In the Beginning 3
Chapter 2	The Ministry Begins 15
Chapter 3	Parables, Healings and Miracles 31
Chapter 4	The Sermon on the Mount 43
Chapter 5	Teachings 57
Chapter 6	Toward the Kingdom of God 67
Chapter 7	To Jerusalem for Passover 79
Chapter 8	The Final Events 93

FOREWORD

This is the English translation of the Book of Emet, found in a cave outside of Nazareth in present-day Israel. The book dates from 30 to 40 years after the death of Jesus of Nazareth. It was originally written in Aramaic, the language used at that time in the land of Judea.

The author of the Book of Emet is Jesus' best friend from childhood, Emet son of Chaim. The book tells a significantly different story of the life and death of Jesus than is found in the gospels of the New Testament. Scholars are currently debating its authenticity. In the meantime, it is for you, the reader, to form your own opinion of this book's veracity.

I have added a short introduction at the beginning of each chapter of the Book of Emet to point out the highlights of that chapter. I have also added New Testament citations where appropriate so the studious reader can make comparisons between the gospels of the New Testament and the Book of Emet. [Mt is Matthew; Mk is Mark; Lk is Luke; and Jn is John.]

The full story of the discovery of the Book of Emet and subsequent events are related in my new book, *Sleeping Truth*.

Special thanks to my friend Sebria Diane Yocco, my publicist Deborah Lanore, and Dr. Elizabeth Feldman and who were instrumental in the writing and creation of this book.

If you want to purchase *Sleeping Truth* or be notified about subsequent books (including soon-to-be-released *Rethinking Judaism: What Is Needed in the 21st Century*), please submit your email address to my website at www.martinvesole.com.

Rabbi Martin K. Vesole, Esq.
http://www.martinvesole.com

Chapter One

IN THE BEGINNING

Introduction

This chapter relates the story of the birth of Jesus in a Jewish family, his childhood, and his being called to the service of God.

Mary was without child and prayed to the Lord to grant her a child, and if her prayer was granted, she promised to dedicate the child to the Lord's service. Her prayer was answered and she became pregnant with Jesus, and she kept her promise. Jesus knew from a young age that he was promised to the Lord's service.

The strong personality of Jesus became evident at an early age. He was kind and gentle and very spiritual. He was charismatic and a natural leader, but also a bit of a loner. When he was about 30, he went to be baptized by John the Baptist, who many believed to be the long-awaited Messiah who would free the Jews from the hated Romans. After being baptized, Jesus had a spiritual experience that convinced him that he should help propagate the belief of John that the coming of the Kingdom of Heaven was at hand.

Unlike John the Baptist, who worked alone, Jesus called 12 disciples to help spread the word that the Kingdom of Heaven was about to come in their own day and that the people should prepare. What distinguished Jesus from other would-be Messiahs in those days is that Jesus did not take money for doing miracles and healings.

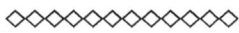

The Birth of Jesus
Mt 1:18

1:1 Joseph and Mary (Miriam) lived in the city of Nazareth in the district of Galilee in the nation of Judea. Joseph knew Mary but Mary was without child.

1:2 Mary prayed to the Lord that she may have a child and promised to dedicate him to the Lord's service.

1:3 And the Lord heard Mary's prayers and opened her womb and gave to Mary and Joseph the child who was named Jesus (Jesse) after the father of Joseph's ancestor, King David.

1:4 And Mary raised Jesus to know that he was promised to the Lord's service and Jesus believed it was so.

1:5 When Mary saw that she was with child, she sang a song to the Lord.

1:6 "My soul glorifies the Lord and my spirit rejoices in God my Savior,

1:7 for He has been mindful of the humble state of His servant

1:8 for the Lord has done great things for me and holy is His Name.

1:9 His mercy extends to those who fear Him, from generation to generation.

1:10 He has performed mighty deeds with His arm,

1:11 He has scattered those who are proud in their inmost thoughts.

1:12 He has brought down the mighty and has exalted the humble.

1:13 He has helped his servant Israel, remembering his promise to Abraham our father."

1:14 It came to pass that Jesus grew up to be a kind and gentle and determined lad who was sensitive to the pain and troubles of others.

The Early Years

1:15 He was interested in the world around him and a strong spiritual nature developed within him. He meditated on the words of the Lord night and day.

1:16 In school, Jesus loved to learn about the laws and customs of his people, and his hunger was great to learn more.

1:17 He went to the discussions held by the sages in the city of Nazareth and was a frequent participant.

1:18 His teachers observed the great learning in one so young and asked Jesus to help teach the younger children.

1:19 He often taught by story-telling, which helped the children understand better.

1:20 He was a natural leader and the other children were drawn to him, but sometimes he preferred to be alone.

1:21 He had a close relationship with the Lord that he valued above all things.

1:22 His friends were working people like himself, the sons of fishermen, carpenters, day laborers, farmers, shepherds, even one who was the son of a tax collector.

1:23 His father sought to make Jesus into a carpenter like himself, but Jesus had no skill and no interest in his father's craft. But to please his father, he worked as a laborer in the building trades.

1:24 The work did not fulfill him and he often wandered off for hours at a time thinking and praying.

1:25 He came to be very troubled by the problems and worries of the poor and downtrodden, and he became angry at the elites who oppressed them.

1:26 He discovered as a youth that he had special healing powers which he believed came from God. But he rarely used them for fear of attracting unwanted attention to himself.

1:27 As a descendant from the House of David, and having been promised to the Lord, he was very confident and knew how to direct the actions of those who were with him.

1:28 He waited impatiently for the time that he would be called upon to do something very important in the world.

1:29 He worked to prepare himself for service. He became strong in spirit, filled with wisdom, and the grace of God was upon him.

1:30 His soul grieved greatly over the cruel and merciless world he saw around him

1:31 and he became convinced that God was about to usher in the Kingdom of Heaven when all things would be set right.

1:32 He hoped and expected that, as a son of David, he would play an important role when that great day arrived.

1:33 He observed that those around him were not ready for the arrival of the Kingdom of Heaven

1:34 and believed he needed to warn them to prepare themselves, lest they miss being included in the Kingdom and missing out on eternal life.

John the Baptist
Lk 3:1-20; Mt 3:1-12

1:35 In the fifteenth year of the reign of Tiberius Caesar, when Pontius Pilate was governor of Judea and Herod tetrarch of Galilee, the word of God came to John the Baptist in the desert.

The Book of Emet

1:36 John's clothes were made of camel's hair, and he had a leather belt around his waist. His food was locusts and wild honey.

1:37 He went into all the country around the Jordan River, preaching a baptism of repentance and the forgiveness of sins, saying "Repent, for the Kingdom of Heaven is near.

1:38 As is written in the book of the words of the prophet Isaiah: "Prepare the way for the Lord, make straight paths for him.

1:39 Every valley shall be filled in, every mountain and hill made low. The crooked shall be made straight, the rough ways made smooth.

1:40 And all mankind shall see the salvation of God."

1:41 John said to the multitude that came forth to be baptized by him, "O generation of vipers, who has warned you to flee from the wrath to come?

1:42 Repent! Do not excuse yourselves saying, 'We have Abraham as our father.' For I say to you that out of these stones God can raise up children for Abraham.

1:43 The ax is ready at the root of the trees, and every tree that does not bring forth good fruit will be hewn down and cast into the fire."

1:44 And the people asked him "What should we do then?"

1:45 And he said to them, "He who has two coats should share with him who has none, and the one who has meat should do likewise."

1:46 Tax collectors also came to be baptized and said to him. "Master, what shall we do?"

1:47 And he said to them. "Do not collect any more than you are supposed to."

1:48 And the soldiers came to him and asked, "And what shall we do?"

1:49 He said to them, "Do violence to no man, nor accuse him falsely, and be content with your wages."

1:50 And the people who heard him believed John was the Messiah they had been waiting for.

1:51 People went out to him from Jerusalem and all Judea and the whole region of the Jordan.

1:52 Confessing their sins, they were cleansed and had their sins washed away by him in the Jordan River, as John the Baptist proclaimed:

1:53 "I baptize you on behalf of the Lord with the water of atonement for your repentance."

1:54 And the people felt cleansed of their sins and renewed in their spirit.

1:55 And the Romans became concerned about John's following and plotted against him.

1:56 And when John rebuked Herod the tetrarch for marrying Herodias, his brother's wife, and all the other evil things he had done, Herod locked John up in prison.

The Baptism of Jesus
Mt 3:13-17; Mk 1:9-11; Lk 3:21-22; Jn 1:31-34

1:57 When Jesus was 30 years of age, he came from Galilee to the Jordan to learn from John and he was greatly inspired by his teachings.

1:58 And when he felt ready, he asked John to baptize him in the River Jordan, and John did so baptize him.

1:59 As soon as Jesus was baptized, and he went up out of the water, he saw heaven open, and felt the Spirit of God descend like a dove upon him.

1:60 And from that time forth, Jesus knew he was called by the Lord to join in the work of John the Baptist, and to prepare the people for the imminent coming of the Kingdom of Heaven.

The Calling of the First Disciples
Mt 4:18-22; 9:9-13;Mk 1:16-20; 2:14-17;Lk 5:2-11, 37-32; Jn 1:35-42

1:61 One day as Jesus was standing by the Sea of Galilee with the people crowding around him and listening to the word of God,

1:62 he saw two boats standing by the lake, left there by the fishermen, who were washing their nets.

1:63 He got into one of the boats, which was Simon's, also called Peter, and his brother Andrew, and asked them to put out a little from shore.

1:64 Then he sat down and taught the people from the boat.

1:65 When he had finished speaking, he said to Peter, "Put out into deep water, and let down your nets for a catch."

1:66 Peter answered, "Master, we have toiled all night and have caught nothing. Nevertheless, at your word, I will let down the nets."

1:67 When they had done so, they caught such a large number of fish that their nets broke.

1:68 So they called their partners in the other boat to come and help them, and they came and filled both boats so full that they began to sink.

1:69 When Peter saw this, he fell at Jesus' knees and said, "Depart from me, Master, for I am a sinful man!"

1:69 When Peter saw this, he fell at Jesus' knees and said, "Depart from me, Master, for I am a sinful man!"

1:70 For he and all his companions were astonished at the quantity of fish they had taken, and so were James and John, the sons of Zebedee, who were Peter's partners.

1:71 Then Jesus said to Peter, "Fear not; from now on you will catch men instead of fish."

1:72 When they pulled their boats up to the shore, they forsook all and followed him.

1:73 As Jesus went on from there, he saw a tax collector named Levi, also called Matthew, sitting at the custom house. "Follow me," he told him, and Matthew got up and followed him.

1:74 While Jesus was having dinner at Matthew's house, many tax collectors and sinners came and ate with him and his disciples.

1:75 A town official asked his disciples, "Why does your teacher eat with tax collectors and sinners?

1:76 On hearing this, Jesus said, "They who are healthy do not need a physician, but rather they who are sick.

1:77 But go and learn what this means: 'I desire mercy, not sacrifice.' For I have not come to call the righteous, but the sinners to repentance."

Appointing the Twelve Apostles
Mt 10:1-4; Mk 3:13-19; Lk 6:12-16

1:78 Jesus went up on a mountain to pray, and he prayed all night, and in the morning he called to him those he wanted as disciples, and they came to him.

1:79 And he chose twelve of them as apostles—that they might be with him and that he might send them out to preach the Kingdom of God
1:80 and gave them authority to drive out evil spirits and to heal every disease and sickness.

1:81 These are the names of the twelve apostles: Simon (who is also called Peter) and Andrew his brother; James son of Zebedee, and his brother John;

1:82 Philip and Bartholomew; Thomas and Levi (who is also called Matthew) the tax collector; James son of Alpheus, and Thaddeus; Simon the Zealot and Judas Iscariot.

Sending Them Out With Instructions
Mt 10:5-42; Mk 6:7-13;Lk 9:1-6, 9:49-50, 10:4-24

1:83 These twelve Jesus sent out with the following instructions: "Do not go among the Gentiles or enter any city of the Samaritans.

1:84 Go rather to the lost sheep of the house of Israel for they are the ones our Father in heaven sent me to help.

1:85 As you go, preach this message: 'The Kingdom of Heaven is at hand.'
1:86 Heal the sick, raise the dead, cleanse those who have leprosy, and drive out demons. Freely you have received, and freely you shall give."

1:87 Then he gave them these additional instructions: "Take nothing for the journey except a staff—no bread, no bag, no money in your belts. Wear sandals but not an extra coat.

1:88 Whatever city or village you enter, enquire who in it is worthy and there stay at his house until you leave.

1:89 When you enter a house, give it your greeting. If the home is worthy, let your peace come upon it. If it is not worthy, let your peace return to you.

1:90 If anyone will not welcome you or listen to your words, shake the dust off your feet when you leave that house or city, as a testimony against them.

1:91 I am sending you out like sheep among wolves. Therefore be as shrewd as snakes and as harmless as doves.

1:92 When you are persecuted in one place, flee to another. I tell you the truth, you will not finish going through the cities of Israel before the Kingdom of Heaven comes.

1:93 A student is not above his teacher, nor a servant above his master. It is enough for the student to be like his teacher, and the servant like his master.

1:94 What I tell you in darkness, speak in the light; what is whispered in your ear, proclaim from the rooftops.

1:95 Do not be afraid of those who kill the body but cannot kill the soul. Rather, be afraid of the one who can destroy both soul and body in hell.

1:96 Are not two sparrows sold for a shekel? Yet not one of them will fall to the ground apart from the will of your Father.

1:97 And even the very hairs of your head are all numbered. So don't be afraid; you are worth more than many sparrows.

1:98 He who receives you receives me, and he who receives me receives the One who sent me.

1:99 Anyone who receives a prophet because he is a prophet will receive a prophet's reward,

1:100 and anyone who receives a righteous man because he is a righteous man will receive a righteous man's reward."

1:101 After Jesus had finished instructing his twelve apostles, he went on from there to teach and preach in the towns of Galilee.

1:102 And the apostles went out and preached that people should repent.

1:103 They drove out many demons and anointed many sick people with oil and healed them.

1:104 "Master," said John, "we saw a man driving out demons in your name and we stopped him, because he is not one of your followers."

1:105 "Do not stop him," Jesus said, "for he that is not against us is for us."

The Workers Are Few
Mt 9:35-38; Lk 10:1-3

1:106 Jesus went through all the towns and villages, teaching in their synagogues, preaching that the Kingdom of Heaven is near and healing every disease and sickness.

1:107 When he saw the crowds, he had compassion on them, because they were helpless, like sheep without a shepherd.

1:108 Then he said to his disciples, "The harvest is plentiful but the workers are few.

1:109 Let us ask the Lord of the harvest, therefore, to send out workers into His harvest field."

1:110 After this Jesus appointed seventy others and sent them two by two ahead of him to every city and place where he was about to go.

1:111 "Go! I am sending you out like lambs among wolves."

1:112 And he gave the seventy the same instructions he gave to the twelve.

Chapter Two

THE MINISTRY BEGINS

Introduction

Jesus initially became known as a healer and exorcist and it was in that capacity that he began to achieve a following, and people flocked to him wherever he went. As his popularity began to grow he started to teach them the unique things he had to say. His primary message was that the Kingdom of Heaven was at hand (meaning the Messiah would come) and that they would see it in their own lifetimes.

Jesus often disagreed with the predominant Jewish political and religious parties of his day, the Sadducees and the Pharisees. He thought they were hypocrites, preaching one thing and doing another, and he called them out on it. Contrary to popular belief, Jesus did not disagree with them about the letter of the law. He was just as observant as they were, possibly even more observant than many of them. His quarrel with them primarily concerned form over matter. He looked to the meaning and purpose of the religious law, whereas they seemed to look at the form of it. So, for example, in one episode they criticized him for healing people on the Sabbath because it was supposed to be a day of rest. Jesus believed that healing was a higher tribute to the sanctity of the Sabbath than the mere rote observance of it.

Jesus Heals the Sick

Mt 4-23-25; 8:14-16; Mk 1:29-34; Lk 4:38-41

2:1 Jesus went throughout Galilee, teaching in synagogues, preaching that the Kingdom of Heaven is near, and healing diseases and sicknesses among the people.

2:2 And his fame spread throughout the region and people brought to him those who were sick with various diseases and pains, the demon-possessed, and the paralyzed, and he healed them.

2:3 People came to him from Galilee, Decapolis, Jerusalem, Judea and the region across the Jordan.

2:4 When Jesus went into Peter's house, he saw Peter's mother lying in bed with a high fever. He touched her hand and the fever left her, and she got up and began to serve unto them.

2:5 At sunrise, the people brought to Jesus those who had various kinds of sickness, and laying his hands on each one, he healed them.

2:6 When evening came, those who were demon-possessed were brought to him, and he drove out the evil spirits from them.

Jesus and Beelzebub

Mt 12:25-29; Mk 3:23-27; Lk 11:17-28

2:7 Then they brought him a demon-possessed man who was blind and mute, and Jesus healed him, so that he could both talk and see.

2:8 And the onlookers were astonished and said, "Could this man be the Messiah we've been waiting for?"

2:9 But others said, "It is only by Beelzebub, the prince of demons, that this fellow drives out demons."

The Book of Emet

2:10 So Jesus called them and spoke to them in parables: "How can Satan drive out Satan?

2:11 If a Kingdom is divided against itself, that Kingdom cannot stand.

2:12 If a house is divided against itself, that house cannot stand.

2:13 If Satan drives out Satan, he is divided against himself. How then can his Kingdom stand?

2:14 And if I drive out demons by Beelzebub, by whom do your people drive them out? So then, they will be your judges.

2:15 But if I drive out demons by the spirit of God, then the Kingdom of God has come unto you.

2:16 When a strong man guards his own house, his possessions are safe.

2:17 But if someone stronger attacks and overpowers him, he takes away the armor in which the man trusted and divides up the spoils.

2:18 And so I tell you, every sin and blasphemy will be forgiven, but the blasphemy against God will not be forgiven.

2:19 Make a tree good and its fruit will be good, or make a tree bad and its fruit will be bad, for a tree is known by its fruit.

2:20 The good man brings good things out of the good stored up in him, and the evil man brings evil things out of the evil stored up in him.

2:21 But I say to you that men will have to give account for every evil word they have spoken on the day of judgment.

2:22 For by your words you shall be absolved, and by your words you shall be condemned."

2:23 As Jesus was saying these things, a woman in the crowd called out, "Blessed is the mother who gave you birth and nursed you."

2:24 He replied, "Blessed rather are those who hear the word of God and obey it."

A Blind Beggar Receives His Sight
Lk 18:35-43; Mt 20:29-34; Mk 10:46-52

2:25 As Jesus was on the way to Jericho, a blind man was sitting by the roadside begging.

2:26 When he heard the crowd going by, he asked what was happening.

2:27 They told him, "Jesus of Nazareth is passing by."

2:28 He called out, "O Jesus, great healer, have mercy on me!"

2:29 Those who went before Jesus rebuked the beggar and told him to hold his peace, but he cried all the more, "Master, have mercy on me!"

2:30 Jesus stopped and ordered that the man be brought to him and when he came near, Jesus asked him,

2:31 "What do you want of me?" And the blind man asked to have his sight restored.

2:32 Jesus said to him, "Receive your sight; your faith has healed you."

2:33 Immediately the beggar received his sight and became a follower of Jesus, glorifying God. When all the people saw it, they also gave praise to God.

The Healing of a Deaf and Mute Man
Mk 7:31-37

2:34 Then Jesus went down to the Sea of Galilee.

2:35 And the people brought to him a man who was deaf and had a stuttered speech, and they beseeched him to place his hand on the man.

2:36 And Jesus took him aside from the crowd and put his fingers into the man's ears, and then he spit and touched the man's tongue.

2:37 He looked up to heaven and said to him, "Ephphatha!" (which means, "Be opened!").

2:38 And straightaway, the man's ears were opened, his tongue was loosened, and he began to speak plainly.

2:39 The people were astonished, saying. "He makes both the deaf to hear and the dumb to speak."

A Dead Girl and a Sick Woman
Mk 5:21-43; Lk 8:40-56; Mt 9:18-26

2:40 When Jesus had again crossed over by boat to the other side of the lake, a group was waiting for him and gathered around him.

2:41 Then one of the rulers of the synagogue, named Jairus, saw Jesus and fell at his feet and pleaded with him,

2:42 "My young daughter is at the point of death. Please come and put your hands on her so that she will be healed and she will live."

2:43 So Jesus went with him and many people followed him and thronged around him.

2:44 And a woman was there who had a disease causing her to be bleeding for twelve years.

2:45 She had suffered many things with many physicians, and although she had spent all she had, instead of getting better she grew worse.

2:46 When she heard about Jesus, she came up behind him in the crowd and touched his garment, for she thought, "If I just touch his clothes, I will be healed."

2:47 And straightaway the fountain of her blood was dried up and she felt in her body that she was healed of that plague.

2:48 And Jesus immediately realized that power had gone out from him. He turned around in the crowd and asked, "Who touched my clothes?"

2:49 And his disciples answered "You see the people crowding against you and yet you can ask, 'Who touched me?'" But Jesus kept looking around to see who had done it.

2:50 Then the woman, trembling with fear, came and fell down before him and told him the truth.

2:51 He said to her, "Daughter, your faith has healed you. Go in peace and be freed from your plague."

2:52 While Jesus was still speaking, some men came from the house of Jairus, the synagogue ruler. "Your daughter is dead," they said to him. "Why bother the teacher any more?"

2:53 Then Jesus told the synagogue ruler, "Be not afraid, only believe, and she will be healed."

2:54 He did not let anyone follow him except Peter and James and John the brother of James.

2:55 And he went into the house of the synagogue ruler, and he saw a tumult, with people weeping and wailing loudly.

2:56 He went in and said to them, "Why all this ado and weeping? The child is not dead but is sleeping."

2:57 And they laughed at him scornfully. But he put them all out, and then he took the little girl's father and mother and the disciples who were with him, and went in to where she was laying.

2:58 He took her by the hand and said to her, "Talitha cumi!" (which means, "Young lady, arise!").

2:59 Her spirit immediately returned and she stood up and walked around. Then Jesus told them to give her something to eat.

2:60 And those who had laughed at him were greatly astonished.

The Healing of the Demon-Possessed Man
Mk 5:1-20; Lk 8:26-39; Mt 8:28-34

2:61 They went across the lake to the region of the Gadarenes, which is near Galilee. When Jesus got out of the boat, a man who was possessed by demons came from the tombs to meet him.

2:62 For a long time this man had not worn clothes or lived in a house, but had lived in the tombs, and no one could bind him, not even with chains.

2:63 For he had often been bound with chains and fetters hand and foot, but he tore the chains apart and broke the fetters off his feet. No one was strong enough to subdue him.

2:64 And always, night and day, he was in the mountains and the tombs, crying and cutting himself with stones.

2:65 But when he saw Jesus from afar, he ran and fell on his knees in front of him.

2:66 And he cried with a loud voice, "I am of no concern to you, Jesus. Swear by God that you won't torment me!"

2:67 Then Jesus asked him, "What is your name?" And he answered, "My name is Legion, for we are many."

2:68 And he begged Jesus again and again not to send them out of this world.

2:69 Now there was a large herd of about 2,000 pigs feeding on a nearby hillside.

2:70 The demons begged Jesus, "Send us into the pigs; that we may enter into them."

2:71 And Jesus gave them leave, and the evil spirits went out and went into the pigs.

2:72 And the pigs suddenly rushed down the steep bank into the sea and were drowned.

2:73 Those tending the pigs fled and told this story in the city and in the country, and the people went out to see what had happened.

2:74 When they came to Jesus, they saw the man who had been possessed by the legion of demons sitting there, being clothed and in his right mind; and they were afraid.

2:75 Those who had seen it told the people what had happened to the demon-possessed man and the pigs.

2:76 Then the people began to plead with Jesus to leave their region.

2:77 As Jesus was getting into the boat, the man who had been demon-possessed begged to go with him.

2:78 Jesus refused him, saying, "Go home to your friends and tell them what great things the Lord has done for you, and how he has had compassion on you."

2:79 So the man went away and told all over town what great things Jesus had done for him through the Lord.

The Healing of the Centurion's Servant
Mt 8:5-13; Lk 7:1-10

2:80 When Jesus was in Capernaum, a Roman centurion came to him, asking for help.

2:81 "Master," he said, "my servant lies at home paralyzed and is grievously tormented."

2:82 Jesus said to him, "I will come and heal him."

2:83 The centurion replied, "Master, I am not worthy to have you come under my roof. But just speak the word, and my servant will be healed.

2:84 For I myself am a man of authority, with soldiers under me. I tell this one, 'Go,' and he goes; and that one, 'Come,' and he comes. I say to my servant, 'Do this,' and he does it."

2:85 When Jesus heard this, he marveled and said to those following him, "I tell you the truth, I have not found anyone in Israel with such great faith."

2:86 Then Jesus said to the centurion, "Go! It will be done just as you believed it would." And his servant was healed at that very hour.

The Faith of the Canaanite Woman
Mt 15:21-28; Mk 7:24-30

2:87 Leaving that place, Jesus was approached by a Canaanite woman who lived in the coastal region to the west.

2:88 She cried out, "Master, have mercy on me! My daughter is suffering terribly from demon-possession."

2:89 But he did not answer her. And his disciples came to him and urged him, "Send her away, for she keeps crying after us."

2:90 He answered, "I am sent only to the lost sheep of the house of Israel."

2:91 The woman came and knelt before him. "Master, help me!" she cried.

2:92 He replied, "It is not right to take the children's bread and cast it to dogs."

2:93 "Yes, Master," she said, "yet the dogs eat the crumbs that fall from their masters' table."

2:94 Then Jesus answered, "Woman, great is your faith! It will be as you wish." And her daughter was healed from that very hour.

Jesus Goes to the Feast of Tabernacles
Jn 7:2-18

2:95 When the Feast of Tabernacles for Sukkot arrived, Jesus' younger brothers said to him, "You ought to leave here and go to Jerusalem, so that the people there may see the miracles you do.

2:96 No one who seeks to be known openly acts in secret. Since you are doing these things, show yourself to the world."

2:97 After his brothers had left for the Feast, he went also, not publicly, but in secret.

2:98 About halfway through the Feast Jesus went up to the Temple in Jerusalem and began to teach.

2:99 The people were amazed and asked, "How did this man get such learning without studying at our best schools?"

2:100 Jesus answered, "My teaching is not my own. It comes from He who sent me.

2:101 If anyone chooses to do God's will, he will find out whether my teaching comes from God or whether I speak on my own.

2:102 He who speaks on his own seeks his own glory, but he who works for the glory of God is a man of truth."

Woe Unto the Hypocrites

Mt 23:1-39; Mk 12:38-39; Lk 13:34-35, 20:45-46

2:103 Then Jesus said to those who came to hear his teachings:

2:104 "The teachers of the law sit in Moses' seat and they tell you what to observe and do.

2:105 But do not do what they do, for they do not practice what they preach.

2:106 They put heavy burdens on men's shoulders, but they themselves are not willing to lift a finger to move them.

2:107 Everything they do is done for men to see: They make their phylacteries wide and the tassels on their garments long;

2:108 They like to have the most important seats in the synagogues and be greeted in the marketplaces, and have men call them 'Lord.'

2:109 But you are not to be called 'Lord,' for there is only one God and you are all brothers. The greatest among you are meant to be His servant.

2:110 For whoever exalts himself will be humbled, and whoever humbles himself will be exalted.

2:111 Woe to you, teachers of the law, you hypocrites! You shut the Kingdom of Heaven in men's faces. You yourselves can not enter, nor will you let those enter who are trying to go in.

2:112 Woe to you, teachers of the law, you hypocrites! You travel over land and sea to win a single convert, and when he becomes one, you make him feel lesser for it unless he does things exactly the way you do.

2:113 Woe to you, teachers of the law, you hypocrites! You give a tenth of your spices—mint, anise and cumin.

2:114 But you have neglected the more important matters of the law—justice, mercy and faith. You should have practiced the latter, without neglecting the former.

2:115 You blind guides! You strain out a gnat but swallow a camel.

2:116 Woe to you, teachers of the law, you hypocrites! You clean the outside of the cup and the platter, but inside they are full of greed and excess.

2:117 First clean what is inside the cup and platter, and then the outside also will be clean.

2:118 Woe to you, teachers of the law, you hypocrites! You make others do the work that needs to be done while you live off their alms so you can study. Our Father did not give us the law for such a purpose.

2:119 On the outside you appear as righteous but on the inside you are full of hypocrisy and iniquity.

2:120 Woe to you, teachers of the law, you hypocrites! You build tombs for the prophets and decorate the graves of the righteous.

2:121 And you say, 'If we had lived in the days of our forefathers, we would not have taken part with them in shedding the blood of the prophets.'

2:122 So you are witnesses against yourselves that you are the children of those who killed the prophets.

2:123 O Jerusalem, Jerusalem, you who kill the prophets and stone those sent to you,

2:124 how often the Lord has longed to gather your children together, as a hen gathers her chicks under her wings, but you were not willing.

2:125 You strive against each other and your house is left to you desolate.

2:126 For I tell you, you will not see the like of me again until you say, 'Blessed is he who comes in the name of the Lord.'"

The Widow's Offering
Mk 12:41-44; Lk 21:1-4

2:127 Jesus sat down opposite the place where the offerings were put and watched how the people put their money into the Temple treasury. Many of those who were rich put in large amounts.

2:128 Then a poor widow came and put in two very small coins, worth only a fraction of a shekel.

2:129 Calling his disciples to him, Jesus said, "I tell you the truth, this poor widow has put more into the treasury than all the others.

2:130 They all gave out of their abundance; but she, out of her poverty, put in all she had to live on."

Observation of the Sabbath
Mt 12:1-8; Mk 2:23-28; Lk 6:1-5

2:131 After the conclusion of the Sukkot feasts, Jesus and the disciples who were with him returned to Galilee.

2:132 One day they were walking through the grainfields on the Sabbath. His disciples were hungry and began to pick some heads of grain and eat them.

2:133 When the elders heard about this, they said to him, "Look! Your disciples are doing what is unlawful on the Sabbath."

2:134 He answered, "Haven't you read what David did when he and his companions were hungry?

2:135 He entered the house of God, and he and his companions ate the consecrated bread, which the law said was reserved only for the priests.

2:136 If you had known what these words mean, 'I desire mercy, not sacrifice,' you would not have condemned the innocent.

2:137 The Sabbath was made for man, not man for the Sabbath."

Healing on the Sabbath

Mt 12:9-14; Mk 3:1-6;Lk 6:6-11, 13:10-17

2:138 Later he went into a nearby synagogue and a man with a shriveled hand was there.

2:139 So the elders asked him, "Is it then lawful to heal on the Sabbath?"

2:140 He said to them, "If any of you has a sheep and it falls into a pit on the Sabbath, will you not take hold of it and lift it out?

2:141 How much more valuable is a man than a sheep! Therefore it is lawful to do good deeds on the Sabbath."

2:142 Then he said to the man, "Stretch forth your hand." So he stretched it out and it was completely restored, just like the other hand.

2:143 On another Sabbath Jesus was teaching in one of the synagogues, and a woman was there who had been bent over for eighteen years and could not straighten herself up.

2:144 When Jesus saw her, he called her to him and said to her, "Woman, you are set free from your infirmity."

2:145 Then he put his hands on her, and immediately she was made straight and gave thanks to God.

2:146 Then the leader of the synagogue was indignant because Jesus had healed on the Sabbath day and spoke to the congregants, and stirred them up saying:

2:147 "There are six days in which men ought to work. It is good to come and be healed on those days, but not on the Sabbath day."

2:148 Then Jesus said to them, "You are hypocrites! Don't each of you on the Sabbath untie and set free your ox or donkey from the stall and lead it out to give it water?

2:149 Then should not this woman, being a daughter of Abraham, who has been kept bound for eighteen long years, be also set free on the Sabbath day?"

2:150 When he said this, the leader of the synagogue was ashamed, and the people rejoiced for the wonderful thing that Jesus had done.

Chapter Three

PARABLES, HEALINGS AND MIRACLES

Introduction

Jesus' favorite way to teach was through parables, in which he told a story that had a meaning to it. Sometimes the disciples did not understand the meaning and he had to explain it to them. It appears that the crowds he preached to were able for the most part to understand the parables. Using parables, he taught that God's words need a good soil in which to grow, that removing evil weeds allows the good crops to thrive, and that finding the beauty of the kingdom of heaven is worth all of a man's riches.

Jesus found that his message was not welcome everywhere. In his home town of Nazareth, familiarity bred disinterest in his message. In some of the other cities he went to, they didn't take to him despite the miracles he performed there. The life of an itinerant preacher began to wear on him and the disciples. Meanwhile, John the Baptist, his hero, was killed.

During this difficult time, he found solace in the friendship of Mary Magdalene, who he had helped earlier by exorcising demons from her. Contrary to the belief of some, Emet reported that Jesus' relationship with her was very respectful and purely platonic. She became someone he could talk to when he needed to talk to someone. She understood him better than any of the other disciples and he learned he could respect her judgment and advice. When he was absent, Mary's was the voice the disciples listened to about what Jesus would or would not do in particular situations.

The chapter ends with some of Jesus' most famous miracles. On one occasion, he fed 5,000 people with just five loaves of bread and two fishes, and then later that night, he was seen to be walking on water. Then Jesus healed a man with leprosy merely by touching him, and even more amazingly, raised a man called Lazarus from the dead after he had already been entombed.

The Parable of the Sower
Mt 13:1-23; Mk 4:1-20; Lk 8:1-15

3:1 After this, Jesus traveled about from one city and village to another, proclaiming the imminence of the Kingdom of God.

3:2 The twelve apostles were with him, and also some women who had been cured of evil spirits and diseases:

3:3 Mary Magdalene; Joanna the wife of Cuza, the manager of Herod's household; Susanna; and many others.

3:4 These women were helping to support Jesus and the disciples out of their own means.

3:5 A large crowd gathered and Jesus told them many things in parables.

3:6 He told them this parable: "A farmer went out to sow his seed. And when he sowed, some fell by the wayside. Some of it was trampled on, and some was eaten by birds.

3:7 Some fell on stony places, where there was not much earth. Those seeds sprung up quickly, because the soil had no depth.

3:8 But when the sun came up, the plants were scorched because they had no roots and, they withered away.

3:9 And some seeds fell among thorns, and the thorns sprung up and choked them.

3:10 But other seeds fell on good soil and brought forth plentiful and delectable fruit."

3:11 His disciples asked him why he speaks in parables and what this parable meant.

3:12 He said, "The knowledge of the secrets of the Kingdom of God has been given to you, but to others I speak in parables, because though seeing, they do not see; though hearing, they do not hear; and neither do they understand.

3:13 This is the meaning of the parable: The seed is the word of God.

3:14 When anyone hears the message about the Kingdom and does not understand it, the evil one comes and snatches away that which was sown in his heart. This is the seed sown by the wayside.

3:15 Those who receive the seed on stony places are the ones who hear God's word with joy, but they don't have the roots within themselves to sustain it. They believe for a while, but when tribulation and persecution arise, they fall away.

3:16 The seed that fell among thorns stands for those who hear God's word, but they become distracted by life's riches and their souls are choked and do not bear fruit.

3:17 But the seed that falls on good earth stands for those who hear God's word and understand it, and their souls grow and blossom and become the best fruits.

A Prophet Without Honor
Mt 13:54-58; Mk 6:1-6

3:22 When Jesus had finished these healings and teachings, he moved on from there.

3:23 Coming to his hometown, he began teaching the people in the synagogue on the Sabbath, but they were unimpressed.

3:24 "Where did this man get this wisdom and these miraculous powers?" they asked.

3:25 "Isn't this the carpenter's son? Isn't his mother's name Mary, and aren't his brothers James, Joseph, Simon and Judas?

3:26 Aren't all his sisters with us? Where then did this man get all these things?"
3:27 And they were offended by him. But Jesus said to them, "Only in his hometown and in his own house is a prophet without honor."

3:28 And he did not do many miracles there because of their lack of faith.

Jesus' Mother and Brothers
Mt 12:46-50; Mk 3:31-35;Lk 6:16

3:29 While Jesus was still talking to the crowd, his mother and his brothers stood outside, wanting to speak to him.

3:30 Some of the people told him, "Your mother and brothers are standing outside wanting to speak to you."

3:31 He replied to him, "Who is my mother, and who are my brothers?"
3:32 And he looked at the crowd around him and said, "You are my mother and my brothers.

3:33 For whoever shall do the will of God, they are my brothers and my sisters and my mother."

3:34 And Jesus often withdrew to lonely places and prayed.

The Cost of Being a Disciple
Mt 8:19-22, Lk 14:26-33

3:35 Then a scribe came to Jesus and said, "Teacher, I will follow you wherever you go."

3:36 Jesus replied, "Foxes have holes and birds of the air have nests, but I have no place to lay my head."

3:37 One of his disciples said to him, "Master, I want to go with you, but first let me go and bury my father."

3:38 But Jesus told him, "Follow me, and let the dead bury their dead.
3:39 If anyone comes to me and cannot leave his father and mother, his wife and children, his brothers and sisters—yes, even his own life—he cannot be my disciple.

3:40 Suppose one of you wants to build a tower. Will he not first sit down and estimate the cost to see if he has enough money to complete it?

3:41 Because if he lays the foundation and is not able to finish it, all that see it will mock him, saying, 'This man began to build and was not able to finish.'

3:42 Or suppose a king is about to go to war against another king. Will he not first sit down and consider whether he is able with ten thousand men to meet the king that is coming against him with twenty thousand?

3:43 If he is not able, he will send a delegation while the other is still a long way off and will ask for terms of peace.

3:44 So likewise, any of you who does not give up all that he has cannot be my disciple."

Woe on Unrepentant Cities
Mt 11:20-24; Lk 10:12-15

3:45 Then Jesus began to upbraid the cities in which most of his miracles had been performed, because they did not repent.

3:46 "Woe to you, Chorazin! Woe to you, Bethsaida! If the miracles that were performed in you had been performed in Tyre and Sidon, they would have repented long ago, sitting in sackcloth and ashes.

3:47 It will be more bearable for Tyre and Sidon on the day of judgment than for you.

3:48 And you, Capernaum, who believes they are exalted, will be brought down low.

3:49 For if the miracles that were performed in you had been performed in Sodom, it would have remained until this day.

3:50 But I say to you that it will be more tolerable for the land of Sodom in the day of judgment than for you."

Mary Magdalene

3:51 One day in their travels, Jesus and the disciples were in the village of Magdala and Jesus was preaching and healing there.

3:52 And one of the healings he did was to expel demons from a woman named Mary (Miriam). After she was cured, she became a devoted follower and helped supply Jesus and his followers with food and places to sleep.

3:53 She was wise and more learned than most of the women in Judea. Jesus quickly came to recognize her wisdom and devoted soul.

3:54 And they had many talks about theology and philosophy and the nature of the world, as well as things in their daily lives.

3:55 And she came to love him as a leader and he came to love her as a follower and she became the most favored of all the disciples who followed Jesus in his journeys.

3:56 He came to trust her and have great respect for her views and opinions and she was able to comfort him when he became morose,

3:57 and intercede with him when he became vexed at his disciples.

3:58 The other disciples noticed that Jesus loved her more than all the others,

3:59 but they did not become jealous because Jesus and Mary made sure that their actions were beyond reproach.

3:60 Although they often went aside to talk, they made sure that they were within the sight of at least one disciple or follower at all times.

3:61 In this way, no rumors were started and everyone knew that their relationship was proper.

3:62 As Mary came to understand the teachings and thoughts of Jesus, she sometimes was called upon to explain them to the other disciples.

3:63 They came to know that what she had to say was from the heart of Jesus and they learned to trust her.

John the Baptist Beheaded
Mt 14:1-12; Mk 6:14-29

3:64 At that time, Herod the tetrarch heard stories about Jesus, and he said to his servants,

3:65 "This is John the Baptist; he has risen from the dead! That is why miraculous powers show themselves in him."

3:66 Now Herod had arrested John and bound him and put him in prison because of Herodias, his brother Philip's wife, for John said to him: "It is not lawful for you to have her."

3:67 And Herod would have put him to death, but he was afraid of the people, because they considered him a prophet.

3:68 On Herod's birthday, Salome the daughter of Herodias danced for them and pleased Herod. Whereupon he promised with an oath to give her whatever she would ask.

3:69 And she, being instructed by her mother, said, "Give me here on a platter the head of John the Baptist."

3:70 The king pretended to be distressed, but claimed that because of his oath he had to order that her request be granted, and had John beheaded in the prison.

3:71 His head was brought in on a platter and given to the girl, and she brought it to her mother.

3:72 John's disciples came and took his body and buried it. Then they went and told Jesus.

Jesus Feeds Five Thousand
Mt 15:13-21; Mk 6:30-44, 8:1-9

3:73 When Jesus heard this, he was very saddened and went by boat to an isolated place in the desert.

3:74 When the people nearby heard where he was, they came on foot to be by him.

3:75 And when Jesus saw them, he was moved by compassion for them, because they were as sheep not having a shepherd; and he began to teach them many things.

3:76 When evening arrived Jesus' disciples came to him and said, "We are in the desert and the time is now past to send the people away to where they can get food for themselves."

3:77 Jesus answered, "They need not depart; give them something to eat."
3:78 His disciples asked him, "Where could we get enough bread in this remote place to feed such a crowd?"

3:79 "How many loaves do you have?" Jesus asked. "Five," they replied, "and two fishes."

3:80 He told the crowd to sit down on the ground. Then he took the five loaves and the two fishes, and he blessed them.

3:81 Then he broke them and gave them to the disciples to set before the people and they did so.

3:82 They all ate and were filled. Afterwards the disciples picked up twelve basketfuls of broken pieces of bread and fish that were left over.

3:83 The number of those who ate were about five thousand men.

Jesus Walks on the Water
Mt 14:22-35; Mk 6:45-56

3:84 After that Jesus told the disciples to get into the boat and go on ahead of him to the other side, while he blessed the crowd and then dismissed them.

3:85 Then he went further up on the mountainside by himself to pray, for his heart was greatly grieved by the death of John the Baptist, who had been his teacher and inspiration.

3:86 When evening came, he was there alone, and the boat was in the midst of the sea. And he saw them, not making progress against the wind.

3:87 During the fourth watch of the night Jesus went out to them, walking on the lake, lost in prayer.

3:88 When the disciples saw him walking on the lake, they thought they were seeing a ghost and cried out in fear.

3:89 But Jesus heard their cries and said to them: "All is right. It is I! Do not be afraid."

3:90 And he got into the ship with them and the wind ceased.

3:91 When they traversed the rest of the lake, they landed at Gennesaret. When the men of that place recognized Jesus, they sent word to the surrounding country.

3:92 And wherever he went—into villages, cities or countryside—they laid the sick in the streets.

3:93 They begged him to let them touch even the border of his cloak, and all who touched him were healed.

The Man With Leprosy
Mt 8:1-4; Mk 1:40-45;Lk 5:12-15

3:94 A man with leprosy came and knelt before him and said, "Master, if you are willing, you can make me clean."

3:95 Jesus was moved with compassion and reached out his hand and touched the man. "I am willing," he said. "Be clean!" And immediately his leprosy was cleansed.

3:96 And Jesus told him to tell no one what he did for him, but to go to the priest and make an offering to God for his cleansing.

Jesus Raises Lazarus From the Dead
Jn 11:1-44

3:97 Now a man named Lazarus was very sick. He was from Bethany, also the village of Mary and her sister Martha, the sisters of Lazarus.

3:98 They sent word to Jesus, "Master, the one you love is sick unto death." Jesus loved Martha and Mary and Lazarus.

3:99 Then he said to his disciples, "Let us go back to Bethany.

3:100 Our friend Lazarus has fallen asleep, but I am going there to wake him up."

3:101 His disciples replied, "Master, if he sleeps, he will get better."

3:102 Jesus had been speaking of his death, but his disciples thought he meant natural sleep.

3:103 So then he told them plainly, "Lazarus is dead."

3:104 On his arrival, Jesus found that Lazarus had already been put in a tomb.

3:105 Bethany was less than two miles from Jerusalem, and many Jews had come to Martha and Mary to comfort them in the loss of their brother.

3:106 When Martha heard that Jesus was coming, she went out to meet him, but Mary stayed at home.

3:107 "Master," Martha said to Jesus, "if you had been here, my brother would not have died. But I know that even now God will give you whatever you ask."

3:108 Jesus said to her, "Your brother will rise again."

3:109 After he said this, she went back and called to her sister Mary. "The Master has come and is calling for you."

3:110 When Mary heard this, she arose quickly and came to him.

3:111 Now Jesus had not yet come into the town, but he was still at the place where Martha met him.

3:112 When the mourners who had been with Mary in the house, comforting her, noticed how hastily she rose up and went out, they followed her, supposing she was going to the tomb to mourn there.

3:113 When Mary came to where Jesus was and saw him, she fell at his feet and said, "Master, if you had been here, my brother would not have died."

3:114 Jesus grieved openly and it was obvious to all how much Jesus loved Lazarus.

3:115 "Where have you laid him?" he asked and they showed him. It was a cave with a stone laid across the entrance. "Take away the stone," he said.
3:116 Then they took away the stone. And Jesus called in a loud voice, "Lazarus, come forth!"

3:117 The dead man came out, his hands and feet wrapped with graveclothes, and a cloth around his face.

3:118 Jesus said to them, "Take off the bindings and let him go."

Chapter Four

THE SERMON ON THE MOUNT

Introduction

This chapter contains the primary teachings of Jesus, which were given by him in a rather lengthy sermon and teaching on a hill in the Galilee. Many people were there to hear him. Some scholars contend that this is the oldest and most accurate portion of the gospels of the New Testament. Emet agrees with the gospels for the most part, but there are significant differences, particularly in regard to what Jesus says about women and homosexuals and about everyone being a child of God.

The Sermon on the Mount contains some very famous sayings, which many readers will recognize from the vernacular, but may be surprised they came from Jesus. Here is a list of some of those sayings:

"Seek and you will find" – On Prayer
Blessed are the meek for they will inherit the earth" – *The Beatitudes*
"You are the salt of the earth" – *Salt and Light*
"I have come not to abolish them (the Laws) but to renew them" – *The Primacy of the Law*
"Go and be reconciled to your brother" – *Murder, Anger and the Judicial System*
"Anyone who looks at a woman lustfully has already committed adultery with her in his heart" – *Adultery*
"Do not swear at all" – *Oaths*
"If someone strikes you on the right cheek, turn to him the other also" – *Turn the Other Cheek*

"Love your enemies" – Love Your Enemies
"Do unto others as you would have them do unto you" – Love Your Enemies
"The poor will always be with us" – Giving to the Needy
"Our Father Who art in heaven, hallowed be Your name" – How to Pray
"Do not worry about tomorrow, for tomorrow will take care of itself" – Do Not Worry
"Do not judge, lest you will be judged" – Judging Others
"They (false prophets) come to you in sheep's clothing" – A Tree and Its Fruit
"By their fruit you will recognize them" – A Tree and Its Fruit
"Let the little children come to me" – The Little Children

On Prayer
Lk 11:1, 5-13; Mt 7:7-11

4:1 One day Jesus was praying by the Sea of Galilee. When he finished, one of his disciples said to him, "Master, does the Lord answer our prayers?"

4:2 Then he said to them, "Suppose one of you has a friend, and he goes to him at midnight and says,

4:3 'Friend, lend me three loaves of bread, because a friend of mine on a journey has come to me, and I have nothing to set before him.'

4:4 Then the one inside answers, 'Do not bother me. The door is already shut, and my children are with me in bed. I can't get up and give you anything.'

4:5 I tell you, though he will not get up and give him the bread because he is his friend, yet because of the man's boldness he will get up and give him as much as he needs.

4:6 So I say to you: ask and it will be given to you; seek and you will find; knock and the door will be opened to you.

4:7 For everyone who asks receives; he who seeks finds; and to him who knocks, the door will be opened.

4:8 Which of you fathers, if your son asks for bread, will give him a stone; or if he asks for a fish, will give him a snake; or if he asks for an egg, will give him a scorpion?

4:9 If you then, though you are sinful, know how to give good gifts to your children, how much more will your Father in heaven give good things to those who ask Him!"

The Beatitudes
Mt 5:1-10

4:10 Now when he saw the crowds that came to meet him by the Sea of Galilee, he went up on a mountainside and sat down. His disciples came to him, and he said to them:

4:11 "Blessed are the meek, for they shall inherit the earth.

4:12 Blessed are those who mourn, for they shall be comforted.

4:13 Blessed are those who hunger and thirst after righteousness, for they shall be filled.

4:14 Blessed are the merciful, for they shall obtain mercy.

4:15 Blessed are the pure in heart, for they shall see God.

4:16 Blessed are the rich in spirit, for they shall sit with God.

4:17 Blessed are the peacemakers, for they shall be called the children of God.

4:18 Blessed are those who are persecuted for righteousness' sake, for theirs is the Kingdom of Heaven."

4:19 Then he motioned for the crowds to draw near and he began to teach.

Salt and Light
Mt 6:13-16

4:20 "You are the salt of the earth. But if the salt loses its saltiness, how can it be made salty again? It is no longer good for anything, except to be cast out and trampled by the foot of men. So you should keep your salt, whatever may befall you.

4:21 You are the light of the world. A city that is set on a hill cannot be hidden.

4:22 Let your light shine before men, that they may see your good works and glorify your Father who is in heaven."

The Primacy of the Law
Mt 6:17-20

4:23 "Do not think that I have come to destroy the Law or the Prophets. I have not come to destroy them but to renew them.

4:24 I tell you the truth, until heaven and earth pass away, not a letter or a marking will pass from the law.

4:25 Anyone who breaks one of the least of these commandments, and teaches others to do so, will be called least in the Kingdom of Heaven. But whoever shall do them and teach them shall be called great in the Kingdom of Heaven.

4:26 And I tell you this, the oral law and rules of the rabbis do not carry the same weight and are not as binding for you. For unless your righteousness exceeds that of the scribes and the elders, you will never enter the Kingdom of Heaven."

Murder, Anger and the Judicial System
Mt 5:21-26; Lk 12:58-59

4:27 "You have heard that it was said to the people long ago, 'Thou shalt not kill, and anyone who kills will be in danger of God's judgment.'

4:28 But I tell you that anyone who is angry with his brother without just cause will be in danger of the judgment.

4:29 Therefore, if you are offering your gift at the altar and there remember that your brother has something against you, leave your gift there in front of the altar. First go and be reconciled to your brother and then come and offer your gift.

4:30 Agree with your adversary quickly, while you are still with him on the way; because if he takes you to court, the judge may hand you over to the officer, and you may be cast into prison.

4:31 I tell you the truth, you will not get out until you have paid the last penny.

4:32 For the laws almost always favor the rich and powerful, and you by yourself can not defeat them."

Adultery
Mt 5:27-30

4:33 "You have heard that it was said, 'Thou shalt not commit adultery.'

4:34 But I tell you that anyone who looks at a woman lustfully has already committed adultery with her in his heart.

4:35 If your right eye causes you to sin, pluck it out and cast it away. It is better for you to lose one part of your body than for your whole body to be thrown into Gehenna.

4:36 And if your right hand causes you to sin, cut it off and cast it away. It is better for you to lose one part of your body than for your whole body to go into Gehenna."

On Women

4:37 "Eve was given to Adam to keep him company for he was lonely without her.

4:38 Do not think of women as secondary, for they support you and all that is best in you.

4:39 God gave them smaller bodies but greater love. Hearken unto them and do what they say, for the word of God is within them."

Homosexuality

4:40 "You have heard that it was said, 'Do not lie with a man as one lies with a woman; for that is an abomination to the Lord.'

4:41 But I tell you this law was meant to apply only to those who are given to procreate.

4:42 For the Lord made men who lie with men as well as men who lie with women and He loves them both."

Oaths
Mt 5:33-37

4:43 "You have heard that it was said to the people long ago, 'Do not break your oath, but keep the oaths you have made to the Lord.'

4:44 But I tell you, do not swear at all: either by heaven, for it is God's throne; or by the earth, for it is his footstool; or by Jerusalem, for it is the city of the Great King.

4:45 Let your 'Yes' be 'Yes,' and your 'No' be 'No.' Anything more than this comes from evil."

Turn the Other Cheek
Mt 5:38-42, 7:12

4:46 "You have heard that it was said, 'An eye for an eye, and a tooth for a tooth.'

4:47 But I say to you, do not resist an evil person. If someone strikes you on the right cheek, turn to him the other also.

4:48 And if any man will sue you at the law and take your coat, let him have your cloak as well.

4:49 If someone forces you to go one mile, go with him two miles."

Love Your Enemies
Mt 5:43-48; Lk 6:27-38

4:50 "You have heard that it was said, 'Love your neighbor and hate your enemies.

4:51 But I say to you, love your enemies, bless those who curse you, do good to those who hate you, and pray for those who hurt and mistreat you.

4:52 Give to he who asks you, and do not turn away he who would borrow from you.

4:53 So in everything, do unto others as you would have them do unto you, for this sums up the Law and the Prophets.

4:54 If you love those who love you, what credit is that to you? Even sinners love those who love them.

4:55 And if you do good to those who are good to you, what credit is that to you? Even sinners do that.

4:56 And if you lend to those from whom you expect repayment, what credit is that to you? Even sinners lend to sinners, expecting to be repaid in full.

4:57 But love your enemies, do good to them, and lend to them without expecting to get anything back.

4:58 Then your reward will be great, and you will be the children of the Lord, because He is kind to the ungrateful and the wicked.

4:59 He causes his sun to rise on the evil and the good, and sends rain on the righteous and the unrighteous.

4:60 Therefore, be merciful, just as your Father in heaven is merciful."

Giving to the Needy
Mt 6:1-4

4:61 "We are commanded to give to the needy, for the poor will always be with us.

4:62 Take heed not to do give your charity in public, to be seen by others. If you do, you will have no reward from your Father in heaven.

4:63 So when you give to the needy, do not announce it with trumpets, as the hypocrites do in the synagogues and in the streets, so that they will be glorified. They already have their reward.

4:64 But when you give to the poor, do not let your left hand know what your right hand is doing, so that your giving may be in secret. Then your Father, who sees what is done in secret, will reward you openly."

How to Pray
Mt 6:6-15; Lk 11:2-4

4:65 "And when you pray, do not be like the hypocrites, for they love to pray standing in the synagogues and on the street corners to be seen by men. I tell you the truth, they already have their reward.

4:66 But when you pray, go into your room and close the door and pray to your Father secretly. Then your Father, who sees what is done in secret, will reward you openly.

4:67 And when you pray, do not use vain repetitions like the pagans do, for they think the more they say, the more they will be heard.

4:68 Do not be like them, for your Father knows what you need before you ask him.

4:69 This, then, is how you should pray:

4:70 'Our Father Who art in heaven, hallowed be Thy name,

4:71 Thy Kingdom come, Thy will be done on earth as it is in heaven.

4:72 Give us this day our daily bread. Forgive us our trespasses, as we also forgive those who trespass against us.

4:73 And lead us not into temptation, but deliver us from evil.

4:74 For thine is the Kingdom, and the power, and the glory, forever. Amen.'

4:75 For if you forgive men when they transgress against you, your heavenly Father will also forgive you.

4:76 But if you do not forgive men their transgressions, your Father will not forgive your transgressions."

Fasting
Mt 6:16-18

4:77 "When you fast, do not have a sad face as the hypocrites do, for they disfigure their faces to show they are fasting. They already have their reward.

4:78 But when you fast, put oil on your head and wash your face,

4:79 So that it will not be obvious to men that you are fasting, visible only to your Father in secret; and your Father, who sees what is done in secret, will reward you openly."

Treasures in Heaven
Mt 6:19- 21

4:80 "Do not store up for yourselves treasures on earth, where moths and rust destroy, and where thieves break in and steal.

4:81 But store up for yourselves treasures in heaven, where moths and rust do not destroy, and where thieves do not break in and steal.

4:82 For where your treasure is, there your heart will be also."

The Light of the Body
Lk 11:33-36; Mt 6:22-23

4:83 "No one who lights a candle puts it in a secret place. Rather he puts it on a candlestick, so that those who come in may see the light.

4:84 The light of the body is the eye. Therefore, if your eye reflects your God-given soul, your whole body will be full of light.

4:85 But if your eye reflects the evil side, your whole body will be full of darkness. If then the light within you is darkness, how great is that darkness!

4:86 Take heed, therefore, that the light within you is not darkness.

4:87 If your whole body is full of light, and no part of it is dark, the whole will be full of light, as when the bright shining of a candle shines light on you."

Do Not Worry
Mt 6:25-34; Lk 12:22-34

4:88 "Do not worry about your life, what you will eat or drink; or about your body, or what you will wear.

4:89 Is not life more important than food, and the body more important than clothes?

4:90 Look at the birds of the air; they do not sow or reap or store food away in barns, and yet your heavenly Father feeds them. Are you not much more important than they?

4:91 Who of you by worrying can add a single inch to your height?

4:92 And why do you worry about clothes? See how the lilies of the field grow. They do not labor or spin.

4:93 Yet I tell you that even Solomon in all his glory was not arrayed like one of these.

4:94 If that is how God clothes the grass of the field, which is here today and tomorrow is cast into the fire, how much more will He clothe you, O ye of little faith?

4:95 So do not worry, saying, 'What shall we eat?' or 'What shall we drink?' or 'What shall we wear?'

4:96 For the Gentiles seek all these things, and your heavenly Father knows that you need them too.

4:99 But seek first the Kingdom of God, and His righteousness, and all these things will be given to you.

4:100 Do not be afraid, little flock, for your Father has been pleased to give you the Kingdom.

4:101 Sell your possessions and give to the poor.

4:102 Provide satchels for yourselves that will not wear out, a treasure in heaven that will not be exhausted, where no thief comes near and no moth destroys.

4:103 For where your treasure is, there your heart will be also.

4:104 Therefore do not worry about tomorrow, for tomorrow will take care of itself.

4:105 Each day has enough trouble of its own."

Judging Others
Mt 7:1-2; Lk 6:37-40

4:106 "Judge not, and you will not be judged.

4:107 For in the same way you judge others, you will be judged, and with the measure you use, it will be measured to you.

4:108 Condemn not, and you will not be condemned. Forgive, and you will be forgiven. Give, and it will be given to you.

4:109 Do unto others as you would have them do unto you."

4:110 Can a blind man lead a blind man? Will they not both fall into a pit?

4:111 A student is not above his teacher, but everyone who is fully trained will be like his teacher.

The Narrow and Wide Gates
Mt 7:13-14

4:112 "Enter through the narrow gate. For wide is the gate and broad is the road that leads to destruction, and many choose to enter through that one.

4:113 But narrow is the gate and narrow is the road that leads to life, and only a few find it."

A Tree and Its Fruit
Mt 7:15-20; Lk 6:43-46

4:114 "Beware of false prophets. They come to you in sheep's clothing, but inwardly they are ravenous wolves.

4:115 You will know them by their fruits. Do people pick grapes from thornbushes, or figs from thistles?

4:116 Likewise every good tree brings forth good fruit, but a bad tree brings forth evil fruit.

4:117 A good tree cannot bring forth evil fruit, neither can a bad tree bring forth good fruit.

4:118 Therefore, by their fruits you will know them.

4:119 A good man brings good things out of the good stored up in his heart, and an evil man brings evil things out of the evil stored up in his heart.

4:120 For from that which is stored up in his heart comes forth the words of his mouth."

The Book of Emet

The Wise and Foolish Builders
Mt 7:24-27; Lk 6:47-49

4:121 "Everyone who hears these words of mine and follows them is like a wise man who built his house on the rock.

4:122 The rain came down, and the floods came, and the winds blew and beat against that house; but it did not fall, because it had its foundation on the rock.

4:123 But everyone who hears these words of mine and does not follow them is like a foolish man who built his house on sand.

4:124 The rain came down, and the floods came, and the winds blew and beat against that house, and it came crashing down."

We Are All Children of God

4:125 "You have heard it said that I have a special relationship with the Father.

4:126 I tell you the truth, I have been called to a special mission. But we all have missions given to us.

4:127 We all of us have God-given souls and that makes us all children of God. We all have God within us.

4:128 Follow the murmurings of your soul and you will be following the Father and He will love you as much as you need.

The Little Children
Mt 19:13-15, 11:25-30; Mk 10:13-16;Lk 10:21, 18:15-17

4:129 Then little children were brought to Jesus for him to place his hands on them and pray for them. And the disciples rebuked those who brought them.

4:130 But Jesus said, "Suffer the little children come to me, and do not hinder them, for the Kingdom of Heaven belongs to such as these.

4:131 I tell you the truth, whoever will not receive the Kingdom of God like a little child will never enter it."

4:132 And he took the children in his arms, put his hands on them and blessed them.

4:133 At that time Jesus said, "I praise you, Father, Lord of heaven and earth, because You have hidden these things from the wise and learned, and have revealed them to little children.

4:134 Come to me, all you who are weary and burdened, and I will give you rest.

4:135 Take my yoke upon you and learn from me, for I am gentle and humble in heart, and you will find rest for your souls.

4:136 For my yoke is easy and my burden is light."

Chapter Five

TEACHINGS

Introduction

One of Jesus' most controversial teachings is that whoever divorces his or her wife or husband, except for marital infidelity, and then remarries, commits adultery. In those days, one who committed adultery was punished by stoning. On the other hand, he essentially prohibited the punishment for an adulteress, because he said "let the one who is without sin cast the first stone."

At one point he met a rich man who wanted to be sure he would go to heaven after his death. The rich man said that he did all the commandments of the Torah. Jesus said that was wonderful but also asked him to give up all his wealth and join his ministry. The man could not bring himself to give away his wealth and Jesus famously said: "It is easier for a camel to go through the eye of a needle than for a rich man to enter the Kingdom of God." He added that no one can serve two masters; you have to choose between God and money.

There are also some interesting parables in this chapter, most famously the story of the good Samaritan. Samaritans lived in a separate country and were not Jewish. In fact, Jews and Samaritans didn't like each other and didn't get along. So this parable shows that kindness can come from any quarter, even from those who you don't like and who don't like you.

This chapter also includes the story of the sinful woman who washed Jesus' feet with her tears and dried them with her hair. Jesus told her that her faith had saved her and that she should go and live a better life.

Divorce and Adultery
Mt 19:1-9; Mk 10:1-12

5:1 Then Jesus left Galilee and went to the east side of the Jordan River. Many people followed him, and he healed them there.

5:2 A rabbi who was there decided to test him and asked, "Is it lawful for a man to divorce his wife?"

5:3 "Haven't you read," he replied, "that at the beginning God 'made them male and female.'

5:4 And He said, 'For this reason a man will leave his father and mother and cleave to his wife, and the two shall be one flesh.'

5:5 So they are no longer two, but one. Therefore what God has joined together, let not man put asunder."

5:6 Then the rabbi asked, "Why then did Moses command that a man give his wife a writing of divorcement and send her away?"

5:7 Jesus replied, "Moses permitted us to divorce our wives because of the hardness of our hearts. But it was not this way from the beginning.

5:8 I tell you that anyone who divorces his wife, except for marital unfaithfulness, and marries another woman commits adultery. And whoever marries her commits adultery.

5:9 And if she divorces her husband and marries another man, she commits adultery."

5:10 And then he said: "Woe to those who profit from divorce and the unlucky ills of others, for they will surely go to the lowest reaches of hell."

The Adulteress
Jn 8:3-11

5:11 The elders of the community then brought in a divorced woman caught in adultery. They made her stand before the group and said to Jesus,

5:12 "Master, this woman was caught in the very act of adultery. The Torah commands us to stone such a woman. But what do you say?" They were using this question as a test, to see how he would rule.

5:13 But Jesus bent down and started to write on the ground with his finger.

5:14 When they continued asking him, he lifted himself up and said to them,

5:15 "He that is without sin among you, let him be the first to cast a stone at her."

5:16 Again he stooped down and wrote on the ground.

5:17 And when the elders heard this, they left one by one till all were gone, and Jesus was left alone, with the woman still standing there.

5:18 Jesus lifted himself up again and saw none but the woman and asked her, "Woman, where are your accusers? Has no one condemned you?"

5:19 "No one, sir," she said. "Then neither do I condemn you," Jesus declared. "Go now and sin no more."

5:20 And he said to his disciples, "Just because there is a law, it does not follow that she who breaks it should be punished by it.

5:11 It is better to be merciful than strict. When no one is harmed there is no need to take the life of the sinner.

5:12 For our Father is a merciful God and He would rather that the sinner repent than be punished."

The Rich Young Man

Mt 19:16-24; Mk 10:17-25; Lk 18:18-25

5:13 Now a man came up to Jesus and asked, "Good teacher, what good things must I do to have eternal life?"

5:14 "Why do you call me good?" Jesus answered. "No one is good—except God alone. But if you want eternal life, obey the commandments." "Which ones?" the man inquired.

5:15 Jesus replied, "'Do not murder, do not commit adultery, do not steal, do not give false testimony, honor your father and mother, and love your neighbor as yourself."

5:16 "All these I have kept since I was a boy," the young man said. "What do I still lack?"

5:17 Jesus answered, "If you want to be perfect, go and sell all your possessions and give to the poor, and you will have treasure in heaven. Then come follow me."

5:18 When the young man heard this, he went away sad, because he had great wealth.

5:19 Then Jesus said to his disciples, "I tell you the truth, it is hard for a rich man to enter the Kingdom of Heaven.

7:20 It is easier for a camel to go through the eye of a needle than for a rich man to enter into the Kingdom of God."

Who Will Be Saved
Mt 19:25-29; Mk 10:26-30; Lk 18:26-3

5:21 When the disciples heard this, they were taken aback and asked, "Who then can be saved?"

5:22 Jesus looked at them and said, "With man this is impossible, but with God all things are possible.

The Book of Emet

5:23 No one can serve two masters. Either he will hate the one and love the other, or he will be devoted to the one and despise the other.

5:24 You cannot serve both God and money."

5:25 Peter then asked him, "We have left everything to follow you! What then will there be for us?"

5:26 Jesus said to them, "I tell you the truth, at the renewal of all things, when God's messenger sits on his glorious throne, you who have followed me will be rewarded for doing God's work.

5:27 I don't know what will be for us but I do know that our Father loves those who give up everything to do His bidding and His works."

5:28 Then Mary Magdalene asked him, "And what will become of you when the Kingdom of Heaven comes?"

5:29 Jesus said to her, "I have a special relationship with our Father because He has called me to His service and I believe we will continue that relationship in the world to come.

5:30 We will know soon, because the Kingdom of Heaven will surely come in our own day.

5:31 That is why it is so urgent for us to spread the word to prepare our people so they can partake of it.

5:32 Everyone who helps spread the word will be amply rewarded in the world to come."

The Parable of the Good Samaritan
Lk 10:25-37; Mt 22:34-40; Mk 12:28-31

5:33 On another occasion an expert in the law stood up to test Jesus. "Teacher," he asked, "which is the greatest commandment in the Torah?"

5:34 He answered: "'You shall love the Lord your God with all your heart and with all your soul and with all your mind.'

5:35 And the second is 'You shall love your neighbor as yourself.'

5:36 On these two commandments hang all the law and the prophets."

5:37 Then the man asked, "And who is my neighbor?"

5:38 And Jesus said: "A man went down from Jerusalem to Jericho, and fell into the hands of thieves. They stripped him of his clothes, and stabbed him and then went away, leaving him half dead.

5:39 A priest happened to be going down the same road, and when he saw the man, he passed by on the other side.

5:40 So too, a Levite, when he came to the place and saw him, passed by on the other side.

5:41 But a gentile Samaritan, as he traveled, came where the man was; and when he saw him, he had compassion for him.

5:42 And the Samaritan went to him and bandaged his wounds, pouring on oil and wine. Then he put the man on his own donkey, took him to an inn and took care of him.

5:43 The next day he took out two silver coins and gave them to the innkeeper, saying. 'Look after him and when I return, I will repay you if you spend more.'

5:44 Which of these three do you think was a neighbor to the man who fell into the hands of thieves?"

5:45 The man of law replied, "The one who had mercy on him." Jesus told him, "Go and do likewise."

A Brother Who Sins Against You
Mt 18:15-20

5:46 If your brother sins against you, go and tell him his fault between you and him alone. If he listens to you, you have gained your brother.

5:47 But if he will not listen, take one or two others along, so that there are two or three witnesses to establish what was said.

5:48 If he refuses to listen to them, tell it to the sage; and if he refuses to listen even to the sage, treat him as you would a pagan or a tax collector."

The Parable of the Unmerciful Servant
Mt 18:21-35

5:49 Then Peter came to Jesus and asked, "Master, how many times shall I forgive my brother when he sins against me? Up to seven times?"

5:50 Jesus answered, "Not seven times, but seventy times seven.

5:51 The Kingdom of Heaven is like a king who wanted to settle accounts with his servants.

5:52 As he began to do the accounting, a servant was brought to him who owed him ten thousand talents.

5:53 Since he was not able to pay, the master ordered that he and his wife and his children and all that he had be sold to repay the debt.

5:54 The servant fell on his knees before him. 'Lord, have patience with me and I will pay back everything.'

5:55 The king was moved to compassion and forgave the debt.

5:56 But when that servant went out, he found one of his fellow servants who owed him a hundred denarii.

5:57 He grabbed him by the throat, saying 'Pay back what you owe me!

5:58 His fellow servant fell to his knees and begged him, 'Have patience with me, and I will pay back everything.'

5:59 But he refused. Instead, he went off and had the man thrown into prison until he should pay the debt.

5:60 When the other servants saw what had happened, they went and told the king everything that had happened.

5:61 Then the king called the servant in and said to him, 'You wicked servant, I forgave all that debt of yours because you begged me to.

5:62 Shouldn't you have had compassion on your fellow servant just as I had on you?'

5:63 And the king was angered against the wicked servant and had him put in jail until he should pay back all he owed.

5:64 So likewise, our heavenly Father will do to you unless you forgive your brother's sins from your heart.

The Parable of the Rich Miser
Lk 12:13-21

5:65 Someone in the crowd said to him, "Master, tell my brother to divide the inheritance with me."

5:66 Jesus replied, "Who made me a judge or an arbiter between you?"

5:67 Then he said to them, "Take heed and beware of covetousness, for a man's life does not consist in the abundance of the things he owns."

5:68 And he told them this parable: "The ground of a certain rich man produced a good crop. He thought to himself, 'What shall I do, because I have no place to store my crops.'

5:69 Then he said, 'This is what I'll do. I will tear down my barns and build bigger ones, and there I will store all my crops and my goods.

5:70 And I'll say to my soul, 'Soul, you have many goods laid up for many years. Now you can take life easy; eat, drink and be merry.'

5:71 But God said to him, 'You fool! This night your soul will be required from you. Then who will get those things that you have provided?'

5:72 So he who stores up treasures for himself is not rich toward God."

Jesus Anointed by a Sinful Woman
Lk 7:36-50; Mt 26:6-13;Mk 14:3-9; Jn 12:1-8

5:73 Now one of the scribes called Simon invited Jesus to have dinner with him, so he went to Simon's house and sat down to a bounteous table.

5:74 When a woman in that city who had lived a sinful life learned that Jesus was eating at Simon's house, she brought an alabaster jar of perfume,

5:75 and as she stood behind him at his feet weeping, she began to wash his feet with her tears. Then she wiped them with her hair, kissed them and poured perfume on them.

5:76 When Simon saw this, he said to himself, "If this man were a prophet, he would know who is touching him and what kind of woman she is, that she is a sinner."

5:77 Jesus answered him, "Simon, I have something to tell you." "Tell me, Master," he said.

5:78 "Two men owed money to a certain moneylender. One owed him five hundred denarii, and the other fifty.

5:79 Neither of them had the money to pay him back, so he forgave the debts of both. Tell me which of them will love him more?"

5:80 Simon replied, "I suppose the one who had the bigger debt canceled."

5:81 "You have judged correctly," Jesus said.

5:82 Then he turned toward the woman and said to Simon, "Do you see this woman? I came into your house. You gave me no water for my feet, but she has washed my feet with her tears and wiped them with her hair.

5:83 You gave me no kiss, but this woman, from the time I came in, has not stopped kissing my feet.

5:84 You did not anoint my head with oil, but she has anointed my feet with perfume.

5:85 Therefore, I tell you, her sins, which are many, are forgiven, for she loved much. But he who loves little will be forgiven little."

5:86 Then Jesus said to the woman, "Your sins are forgiven. Your faith has saved you; go in peace."

Chapter Six

TOWARD THE KINGDOM OF GOD

Introduction

As his ministry continued, Jesus became more and more focused on the arrival of the Kingdom of Heaven, which he believed would happen very soon, and within the lifetime of most of the people he was preaching to. He urged everyone to be ready, because the Kingdom might come at any hour, but was definitely on its way, and soon.

He told everyone to be dressed and ready. Just as it was before Noah and the flood, people went about their normal lives, unaware of the catastrophe that was about to befall them. Some would be chosen and others would be swept away, he told them. Those who repent would be saved. But he also taught that God is like a shepherd who is concerned about all His sheep, and if even one would be lost, God would be all the happier if it is found and returned to the flock. He loves them all and doesn't want to lose a single sheep.

When the Kingdom of Heaven comes, Jesus taught, class distinctions won't matter. So it is better to treat well the poor along with the successful, for the person who does that would be rewarded. He told those who had talent and who had been given much by God to use those gifts well, because in the Kingdom of Heaven those who did not use wisely what was given them would lose them and their gifts would be given to others.

Perhaps presciently, Jesus warned his followers not to chase false Messiahs. They would hear people tell them the Messiah is here, or no, he is there.

He told them they would know the Messiah by the cataclysmic events that will accompany the Messiah's arrival. It will be as dramatic as Noah's flood. It is ironic that the followers of Jesus declared him the Messiah, because according to Emet, Jesus certainly knew he wasn't, and if he had any doubts about it during his lifetime, he certainly knew he wasn't the Messiah upon his death.

The Day and Hour Unknown
Mt 24:36-42; Mk 13:32-37; Lk 12:35-40

6:1 The disciples came to Jesus and asked him how they would know when the Kingdom of Heaven is coming.

6:2 He replied, "Be dressed and have your lamps burning,

6:3 like men waiting for their master to return from a wedding banquet,

6:4 so that when he comes and knocks they can immediately open the door for him.

6:5 Blessed are those servants whose master finds them ready, even if he comes in the second or third watch of the night.

6:6 If the owner of the house had known at what hour the thief was coming, he would have watched and been ready.

6:7 You also must be ready, because the Messiah will come at an hour when you do not expect him.

6:8 No one knows about that day or hour, not even the angels in heaven. Only God knows.

6:9 As it was in the days of Noah, so it will be at the coming of the Messiah.

:10 For in the days before the flood, people were eating and drinking, marrying and given in marriage, up to the day Noah entered the ark;

The Book of Emet

6:11 and they knew nothing about what would happen until the flood came and took them all away.

6:12 That is how it will be at the coming of the End of Days

6:13 Two men will be in the field; one will be taken and the other left.

6:14 Two women will be grinding at the mill; one will be taken and the other left.

6:15 Keep watch, therefore, because you do not know at what hour the Messiah will come.

6:16 If he comes suddenly, do not let him find you sleeping.

6:17 What I say to you, I say to everyone: 'Watch!' "

The Parable of the Ten Virgins
Mt 25:1-13

6:18 "The Kingdom of Heaven will be like ten virgins who took their lamps and went forth to meet the bridegroom.

6:19 Five of them were wise and five were foolish.

6:20 The foolish ones took their lamps but took no oil with them.

6:21 But the wise ones took oil in their vessels along with their lamps.

6:22 When the bridegroom tarried, they all became drowsy and fell asleep.

6:23 At midnight the cry rang out: 'The bridegroom is coming! Go out to meet him!'

6:24 Then all the virgins arose and trimmed their lamps.

6:25 The foolish ones said to the wise, 'Give us some of your oil; our lamps are gone out.'

6:26 But the wise ones answered 'No, for there may not be enough for both us and you. Instead, go to those who sell oil and buy some for yourselves.'

6:27 And while they were out buying the oil, the bridegroom came. The virgins who were ready went in with them to the wedding and the door was shut.

6:28 Later the others also came asking for the door to be opened for them. But he replied, 'I don't know you.'

6:29 Keep ready, therefore, because you do not know the day or the hour when the Messiah will come."

Repent or Perish
Lk 13:1-9

6:30 Now there were some present at that time who told Jesus about the Galileans whose blood Pontius Pilate had mixed with their sacrifices.

6:31 Jesus answered, "Do you think that these Galileans were worse sinners than all the other Galileans because they suffered this way?

6:32 I tell you, no! But unless you repent, you too will all perish.

6:33 Or those eighteen who died when the tower in Siloam fell on them—do you think they were more guilty than all the others living in Jerusalem?

6:34 I tell you, no! But unless you repent, you too will all perish."

6:35 Then he told this parable: "A man had a fig tree planted in his vineyard, and he came to look for fruit on it, but did not find any.

6:36 So he said to the dresser of the vineyard, 'For three years now I've been coming to look for fruit on this fig tree and haven't found any. Cut it down! Why should it use up the soil?'

The Book of Emet

6:37 And the man replied, 'let it alone this year also, till I dig around it and fertilize it.

6:38 If it bears fruit next year, good! But if not, then we will cut it down.' "

The Parable of the Lost Sheep
Lk 15:1-7; Mt 18:12-14

6:39 Now the tax collectors and sinners were all gathering around to hear him.

6:40 But the elders murmured, "This man welcomes sinners and eats with them."

6:41 Then Jesus told them this parable: "Suppose one of you has a hundred sheep and loses one of them.

6:42 Does he not leave the ninety-nine in the wilderness and go after the one that is lost till he finds it?

6:43 And when he finds it, he is happier about that one sheep than about the ninety-nine that did not wander off.

6:44 In the same way, there is joy in heaven over one sinner who repents, more than the ninety-nine righteous people who need no repentance."

The Tax Collector of Jericho
Lk 19:1-10

6:45 Jesus entered Jericho and was passing through.

6:46 And there was a man named Zacchaeus, who was the chief tax collector and was wealthy.

6:47 He wanted to see who Jesus was, but being a short man he could not, because of the crowd.

6:48 So he ran ahead and climbed a sycamore tree to see him, since Jesus was coming that way.

6:49 When Jesus reached that place, he looked up and saw him and said to him, "Zacchaeus, come down immediately for today I must stay at your house."

6:50 So he came down at once and welcomed him joyfully.

6:51 All the people saw this and began to mutter, "He has gone to be the guest of a sinner."

6:52 But Zacchaeus stood up and said to Jesus, "I give half of my possessions to the poor, and if I have cheated anybody out of anything, I will pay back four times the amount."

6:53 Jesus said to him, "Today salvation has come to this house, because this man, too, is a son of Abraham.

6:54 For God's servant came to seek and to redeem that which was lost."

The Parable of the Workers in the Vineyard
Mt 20:1-16

6:55 He taught the crowd about generosity with another parable. "The Kingdom of Heaven is like a landowner who went out early in the morning to hire laborers to work in his vineyard.

6:56 He agreed to pay them a denarius for the day and sent them into his vineyard.

6:57 About the third hour he went out and saw others standing idle in the marketplace.

6:58 He told them, 'You also go and work in my vineyard, and I will pay you whatever is right.' And they went there.

6:59 He went out again about the sixth hour and the ninth hour and did the same thing.

6:60 About the eleventh hour he went out and found still others standing around. He asked them, 'Why have you been standing here all day long doing nothing?'

6:61 'Because no one has hired us,' they answered. He said to them, 'You also go and work in my vineyard and I will pay you whatever is right.'

6:62 When evening came, the owner of the vineyard said to his steward, 'Call the workers and pay them their wages, beginning with the last ones hired and going on to the first.'

6:63 The workers who were hired about the eleventh hour came and each received a denarius.

6:64 So when those came who were hired first, they expected to receive more. But each one of them also received a denarius.

6:65 When they received it, they began to grumble against the landowner.

6:66 'These men who were hired last worked only one hour,' they said, 'and you have made them equal to us who have borne the burden of the work and the heat of the day.'

6:67 But he answered one of them, 'Friend, I am not being unfair to you. Didn't you agree to work for a denarius?

6:68 Take your pay and go. I want to give the man who was hired last the same as I gave you. For his family needs the wages as much as yours does.

6:69 Don't I have the right to do what I want with my own money? Or are you envious because I am generous?'

6:70 So the last will be first, and the first will be last."

The Parable of the Talents
Mt 25:14-30; Lk 19:12-26

6:71 "The Kingdom of Heaven is like a man going on a journey, who called his servants and entrusted his property to them.

6:72 To one he gave five talents of money, to another two talents, and to another one talent, each according to his ability. Then he went on his journey.

6:73 The man who had received the five talents went and traded them and gained five more.

6:74 So also, the one with the two talents gained two more.

6:75 But the man who had received the one talent went off, dug a hole in the ground and hid his master's money.

6:76 After a long time the master of those servants returned and settled accounts with them.

6:77 The man who had received the five talents brought the other five, saying. 'Lord, you entrusted me with five talents. See, I have gained five more.'

6:78 His master replied, 'Well done, good and faithful servant! You have been faithful with a few things. I will put you in charge of many things. Come and share your lord's happiness!'

6:79 The man with the two talents came and said. 'Lord, you entrusted me with two talents and see, I have gained two more.'

6:80 His master replied, 'Well done, good and faithful servant! You have been faithful with a few things; I will put you in charge of many things. Come and share your lord's happiness!'

6:81 Then the man who had received the one talent came and said, 'Lord, I knew that you are a hard man, reaping where you have not sown and gathering where you have not strawed.

6:82 And I was afraid and went and hid your talent in the earth. See, here is what belongs to you.'

6:83 His master replied, 'You wicked and slothful servant! So you knew that I reap where I have not sown and gather where I have not strawed?

6:84 Well then, you should have given my money to the exchangers, so that when I returned I would have received it back with interest.

6:85 Take the talent from him and give it to the one who has the ten talents.'"

6:86 And Jesus said: "He who has will be given even more, and he will have an abundance. But for he who does not have, even what he has will be taken from him."

Doing Your Duty
Lk 17:7-10

6:87 "Suppose you have a servant plowing or feeding cattle. Would you tell him when he comes in from the field, 'Go and sit down to eat'?

6:88 Would you not rather say, 'Prepare my supper, get yourself ready and serve me while I eat and drink; after that you may eat and drink'?

6:89 Would you thank the servant because he did what he was commanded to do? I think not.

6:90 So you likewise, when you have done everything you were commanded to do, should say, 'We are unworthy servants; we have only done that which was our duty to do.'"

A Seat at the Table
Lk 14:8-24; Mt 22:1-14

6:91 One Sabbath, Jesus went to eat in the house of a prominent teacher of the law.

6:92 When he noticed how the guests picked the places of honor at the table, he told them this parable:

6:93 "When you are invited you to a wedding feast, do not take a place of honor, for a person more distinguished than you may have been invited.

6:94 If so, the host who invited both of you will come and say to you, 'Give this man your seat.' Then, humiliated, you will have to take the least important place.

6:95 But when you are invited, take the lowest place, so that when your host comes, he will say to you, 'Friend, move up to a better place.' Then you will be honored in the presence of all your fellow guests.

6:96 For everyone who exalts himself will be humbled, and he who humbles himself will be exalted."

6:97 Then Jesus said to his host, "When you give a luncheon or dinner, do not invite your friends, your brothers or relatives, or your rich neighbors; if you do, they may invite you back and so you will be repaid.

6:98 But when you give a banquet, invite the poor, the crippled, the lame, and the blind, and you will be blessed.

6:99 Although they cannot repay you, you will be repaid at the resurrection of the righteous."

6:100 When one of those at the table with him heard these things, he said to Jesus, "Blessed is the man who will eat bread in the Kingdom of God."

6:101 Jesus replied: "A certain man was preparing a great banquet and invited many guests.

6:102 And sent his servant to tell those who had been invited, 'Come, for everything is now ready.'

6:103 But they all began to make excuses. The first said, 'I have bought a piece of ground, and I must go and see it. Please have me excused.'

6:104 Another said, 'I have bought five yoke of oxen, and I'm on my way to try them out. Please have me excused.'

6:105 Still another said, 'I just got married, so I can't come.'

6:106 The servant came back and reported this to his master. Then the master of the house became angry and said to his servant, 'Go out quickly into the streets and alleys of the city and bring in the poor, the crippled, the lame, and the blind.'

6:107 Then the servant said, 'Lord, it is done as you commanded, but there is still room.'

6:108 Then the master told his servant, 'Go out into the highways and country roads and urge them to come in, so that my house may be filled.

6:109 I tell you, not one of those men who were invited will get a taste of my banquet.'

6:110 Such a man as this is one who will be invited to eat bread in the Kingdom of God."

Preparing for the Kingdom of God
Lk 17:20-32; Mt 24:37-39

6:111 Once, having been asked by an elder when the Kingdom of God would come, Jesus replied, "The Kingdom of God does not come with outward observation,

6:112 nor will people say, 'Here it is,' or There it is,'

6:113 because the Kingdom of God is also within you."

6:114 Then he said to his disciples, "The time is coming when you will long to see the days of the Messiah, but you will not see them.

6:115 They will say to you, 'Here he is!' or 'There he is!' Do not go after them or follow them.

6:116 For as the lightning, that flashes out of one part of heaven, while the sun shines in another part of heaven, that is how the Messiah will be when he comes.

6:117 Just as it was in the days of Noah, so also will it be in the days of the Messiah.

6:118 People were eating, drinking, marrying and being given in marriage up to the day Noah entered the ark. Then the flood came and destroyed them all.

6:119 It was the same in the days of Lot. People were eating and drinking, buying and selling, planting and building.

6:120 But the day that Lot went out of Sodom, it rained fire and brimstone from heaven and destroyed them all.

6:121 It shall be like this on the day when the Messiah is revealed.

6:122 On that day no one who is on the roof of his house, with his goods inside, should go down to get them. And he who is in the field likewise should not go back.
6:123 Remember Lot's wife!"

Chapter Seven

TO JERUSALEM FOR PASSOVER

Introduction

In the Spring, Jesus pilgrimaged again to Jerusalem, this time for the freedom-celebrating holiday of Passover. When he entered the city, a large crowd of people who had heard of him formed and cheered him. Historians think he was virtually unknown outside of his native Galilee but there were obviously many people in Jerusalem, possibly there for the pilgrimage just like Jesus, who had heard of him and thought well of him. His followers told everyone that Jesus would restore the Kingdom of David and drive out the Romans.

When he got to Jerusalem, Jesus went to the Temple to preach and teach as he had done before. But this time he noticed that the vendors near the Temple who were making change and selling animals for sacrifice were cheating the people. He lost his temper and disrupted their businesses. The vendors were working for the wealthy Romans who had come on the heels of the Roman soldiers who occupied Jerusalem and the rest of Judea. Like most occupiers, the wealthy Romans skimmed off the cream from the top and took the best of the best. Cheating the poor ignorant masses was something they felt entitled to do. When Jesus disrupted their businesses they decided to have him eliminated.

Jesus again prophesied about the coming of the Messiah and again warned everyone not to chase false Messiahs. There will be great upheavals to mark the Messiah's coming, Jesus taught, so that no one would be needing to guess. If those things don't happen, he tells them, then the Messiah claimant is a false one. He also told the famous story of the prodigal son.

The Arrival
Mt 21:1-11; Mk 11:1-10; Lk 19:29-38; Jn 12:12-13

7:1 And Jesus and his followers left Jericho and made their pilgrimage to the Holy City of Jerusalem for the Passover Feasts. As was the custom, they arrived a week before the Feasts so they could be ritually purified.

7:2 A large crowd formed of his followers and others who had heard of Jesus and his teachings and healings and miracles.

7:3 Some went ahead of him shouting, "Hosanna to the Son of David!"

7:4 When the residents of Jerusalem saw the crowds and heard the shouting they asked, "Who is this?"

7:5 They answered, "This is Jesus, the healer from Nazareth in Galilee."

7:6 But those who were followers of Jesus answered, "Blessed is the King who comes in the name of the Lord!"

7:7 "Blessed is the coming Kingdom by the son of David! He will restore our nation and drive out the pagans!"

7:8 Now Herod the tetrarch heard about all that was going on. And he was perplexed, because some were saying that John the Baptist had been raised from the dead,

7:9 others that Elijah had appeared, and still others that one of the prophets of long ago had come back to life.

7:10 But Herod said, "I beheaded John. Who, then, is this I hear such things about?"

7:11 And he sent a messenger to the governor of Judea, Pontius Pilate, and told him to beware of this man Jesus who some of the people were calling King.

Jesus at the Temple
Mt 21:12-17; Mk 11:15-17; Lk 19:45-46; Jn 2:12-16

7:12 Jesus entered the outskirts of the Temple area, where cattle, sheep, and doves for sacrifice were sold

7:13 and Roman moneychangers converted the various currencies into the Roman coins accepted by the vendors.

7:14 And he saw that the people were being cheated by the moneychangers and the vendors and his anger was kindled.

7:15 So he made a whip out of cords, and drove the sheep and the cattle from the Temple area and he scattered the coins of the moneychangers and overturned their tables and also the benches of their associates who were selling doves.

7:16 The astonished onlookers asked him, "Where do you get your authority to do all this?"

7:17 "It is written," he said to them, "'My house will be called a house of prayer,' but they are making it a den of thieves. These pagans are cheating our people and desecrating our holy Temple and making our sacrifices to the Lord unholy."

7:18 Then he invited the blind and the lame among the onlookers to come to him at the Temple, and he healed them.

7:19 But when the cabal of powerful and wealthy Roman merchants who hired the cheating moneychangers and vendors saw the wonderful things he did, and the people shouting his praises in the Temple area, they became angry and afraid.

7:20 "This man will turn the people against us and destroy our businesses," they said.

7:21 And they decided he must be stopped and they conspired against him.

7:22 And Jesus left the Temple and went out of the city to Bethany, where he spent the night.

The Fig Tree Withers
Mt 21:18-22; Mk 11:12-14

7:23 In the morning, as he was on his way back to the city, he was hungry.

7:24 Seeing a fig tree by the road, he went up to it but found nothing on it except leaves, for the fruiting season had not yet begun.

7:25 And his anger was kindled and he said to it, "May you never bear fruit again!" Immediately the tree withered.

7:26 When the disciples saw this, they were amazed. "How did the fig tree wither so quickly?" they asked.

7:27 Jesus replied, "I tell you the truth, if you have faith and do not doubt, not only can you do what was done to the fig tree, but also you can say to this mountain, 'Be removed and cast yourself into the sea,' and it will be done.

7:28 And in all things, whatever you ask for in prayer, believing, you will receive.

7:29 And when you stand praying, if you hold anything against anyone, forgive him, so that your Father in heaven may forgive you your sins."

Paying Taxes to Caesar
Mt 22:15-22; Mk 12:13-17; Lk 20:20-26

7:30 Then some of the priests went out and posed a question to Jesus that had been troubling them.

7:31 "Teacher," they said, "we know you are a man of integrity and that you teach the way of God in truth.

7:32 You aren't swayed by men, because you pay no attention to who they are.

7:33 Tell us then, what is your opinion? Is it right to pay taxes to Caesar or not?"

7:34 And Jesus said, "Show me the coin used for paying the taxes." And they brought him a Roman coin.

7:35 And he asked them, "Whose portrait is this? And whose inscription?"

7:36 "Caesar's," they replied. Then he said to them, "Render unto Caesar what is Caesar's, and to God what is God's."

7:37 When they heard this, they were very impressed and had no more questions. So they left him and went away.

Marriage at the Resurrection
Mt 22:23-32; Mk 12:18-27; Lk 20:27-38

7:38 That same day a group of Sadducees, who didn't believe in resurrection of the dead, came and asked him another question.

7:39 "Teacher," they said, "Moses told us that if a man dies without having children, his brother must marry the widow and have children for his brother.

7:40 Now there were with us seven brothers. The first one married and died, and since he had no children, he left his wife to his brother.

7:41 The same thing happened to the second and third brother, right on down to the seventh.

7:42 And last of all, the woman died also.

7:43 Now then, at the resurrection, whose wife will she be of the seven, since all of them were married to her?"

7:44 Jesus replied, "You err because you do not know the Scriptures nor the power of God.

7:45 At the resurrection people will neither marry nor be given in marriage, but are like the angels of God in heaven.

7:46 Remember God spoke to us through Moses at the burning bush and said, 'I am the God of Abraham, and the God of Isaac, and the God of Jacob.' That means there will be a resurrection and that the righteous dead will rise.

7:47 God is not the God of the dead, but of the living, for to Him all are alive."

The Greatest Commandment
Mk 12:28-34; Mt 22:34-40

7:48 One of the teachers of the law came and heard them debating. Noticing that Jesus had given them a good answer, he asked him,

7:49 "Teacher, which is the greatest commandment in the Torah?"

7:50 "The most important one," answered Jesus, "is this:

7:51 'Hear, O Israel, the Lord is our God, the Lord is One.

7:52 You shall love the Lord your God with all your heart and with all your soul and with all your might.'

7:53 The second is this: 'You shall love your neighbor as yourself.' There are no commandments greater than these.

7:54 On these two commandments hang all the Law and the Prophets."

7:55 "Well said, teacher," the man replied. "You are right in saying that God is one and there is no other but Him.

7:56 To love him with all your heart, with all your understanding and with all your strength, and to love your neighbor as yourself is more important than all burnt offerings and sacrifices."

7:57 When Jesus saw that he had answered wisely, he said to him, "You are not far from the Kingdom of God."

Signs of the End of the Age
Mt 24:1-34; Mk 13:1-30; Lk 21:5-38

7:58 As he went out of the Temple one of his disciples said to him, "Master, see what beautiful stones and buildings are here."

The Book of Emet

7:59 And Jesus answered, "Do you see these great buildings? There will not be left one stone on another; every one will be thrown down."

7:60 As Jesus was sitting on the Mount of Olives, some of the apostles came to him privately and asked, "Tell us, when will this happen, and what will be the sign of the coming of the Messiah and of the end of the age?"

7:61 Jesus answered: "Watch out that no one deceives you.

7:62 For many will come in the Lord's name claiming, 'I am the Messiah,' and they will perform great signs and miracles and will deceive many. Do not follow them.

7:63 For as lightning that comes from the east is visible even in the west, so will be the coming of the Messiah.

7:64 You will hear of wars and rumors of wars, but do not be troubled. Those things must happen, but that will still not be the end.

7:65 Nation will rise against nation, and kingdom against kingdom. There will be famines and earthquakes and pestilences in many places, but these are only the beginnings of the sorrows.

7:66 You must be on your guard. They will lay hands on you and persecute you. You will be handed over to the local councils and flogged in the prisons.

7:67 On account of your faith in the One God you will be prosecuted before rulers and kings.

7:68 Then you will be handed over to be persecuted and put to death, and you will be hated by all nations because you are for your true Father in heaven.

7:69 At that time many will turn away from the faith and will betray and hate each other, and many false prophets will appear and deceive many people.

7:70 Because of the increase of wickedness, the love of most will grow cold, but he who stands firm to the end will be saved.

7:71 And the coming of the Kingdom of Heaven will be preached in the whole world as a testimony to all nations, and then the end will come.

7:72 When you see Jerusalem being surrounded by armies, you will know that its desolation is near.

7:73 Then let those who are in Judea flee to the mountains, let those in the city get out, and let those in the country not enter the city.

7:74 How dreadful it will be in those days for pregnant women and nursing mothers! There will be great distress in the land and wrath against our people.

7:75 They will fall by the sword and will be taken as prisoners.

7:76 Jerusalem will be trampled on by the Gentiles until the times of the Gentiles are fulfilled.

7:77 Immediately after the tribulation of those days the sun will be darkened, and the moon will not give her light; the stars will fall from heaven, and the powers of the heavens will be shaken.

7:78 And then will appear the sign of the Messiah in heaven and all the tribes of the earth will mourn,

7:79 and they will see the Messiah coming in the clouds of heaven with power and great glory.

7:80 And God will send His angels with the great sound of the shofar, and they will gather His elect from the four winds, from the ends of the earth to the ends of the heavens.

7:81 Now learn this lesson from the fig tree: As soon as its twigs get tender and its leaves come out, you know that summer is near.

7:82 Even so, when you see all these things, you know that it is near, right at the door.

7:83 I tell you the truth, this generation will certainly not pass away until all these things have happened."

7:84 Each day Jesus was teaching at the Temple, and each evening he went out to spend the night on the Mount of Olives,

7:85 and the people came early in the morning to hear him at the Temple.

The Authority of Jesus Questioned
Mt 21:23-27; Mk 11:27-33; Lk 20:1-8

7:86 The next day when Jesus returned to the Temple, some of the priests from the Temple came to him, and said,

7:87 "By what authority do you do these things? And who gave you this authority?"

7:88 Jesus replied, "I will also ask you one question. If you answer me, I will tell you by what authority I do these things.

7:89 John's authority to do baptisms—where did it come from? Was it from heaven or from men?"

7:90 They discussed it among themselves and said, "If we say, 'From heaven,' he will ask, 'Then why didn't you believe him?'

7:91 But if we say, 'From men'—we fear the people, for they all hold that John was a great prophet."

7:92 So they answered Jesus and said, "We cannot tell."

7:93 Then he said, "Neither will I tell you by what authority I do these things."

Helping the Poor and Needy
Mt 25:31-46

7:94 "When the Messiah comes in his glory, and all the angels with him, he will sit upon the throne of his glory.

7:95 All the nations will be gathered before him, and he will separate the people one from another, as a shepherd separates the sheep from the goats.

7:96 He will put the righteous on his right and the unrighteous on his left.

7:97 Then the King will say to those on his right, 'Come, you who are blessed by God; inherit the Kingdom prepared for you since the creation of the world.

7:98 For I was hungry and you gave me meat, I was thirsty and you gave me drink, I was a stranger and you took me in,

7:99 I was naked and you clothed me, I was sick and you looked after me, I was in prison and you came to visit me.'

7:100 Then the righteous will answer him, 'Lord, when did we see you hungry and feed you, or thirsty and give you something to drink?

7:101 When did we see you a stranger and took you in, or naked and clothe you?

7:102 When did we see you sick or in prison and go to visit you?'

7:103 The King will reply, 'I tell you the truth, whatever you did for one of the least of these brothers of mine, you did for me.'

7:104 Then he will say to those on his left, 'Depart from me, for you have cursed yourselves by your actions.

7:105 For I was hungry and you gave me no meat, I was thirsty and you gave me no drink,

7:106 I was a stranger and you did not take me in, I was naked and you did not clothe me, I was sick and in prison and you did not visit me.'

7:107 They also will answer, 'Lord, when did we see you hungry or thirsty or a stranger or naked or sick or in prison, and did not help you?'

7:108 He will reply, 'I tell you the truth, whatever you did not do for one of the least of these, you did not do for me.'"

The Parable of the Prodigal Son
Lk 15:11-32

7:109 Jesus continued: "There was a man who had two sons.

7:110 The younger one said to his father, 'Father, give me my share of the estate.' So he divided his property between them.

7:111 Not long after that, the younger son got together all he had, set off for a distant country and there squandered his wealth in wild living.

7:112 And when he had spent everything, there was a severe famine in that land, and he began to be in need.

7:113 So he went and hired himself out to a citizen of that country, who sent him to his fields to feed pigs.

7:114 He longed to fill his stomach with the husks that the pigs were eating, but no one gave anything to him.

7:115 Then he came to the realization, 'How many of my father's hired servants have bread enough to spare, and I perish from hunger!

7:116 I will go back to my father and say to him: Father, I have sinned against heaven and against you, and am no longer worthy to be called your son; make me as of your hired servants.'

7:117 So he got up and went to his father. But when he was yet a long way off, his father saw him and had compassion for him; he ran to his son, threw his arms around him and kissed him.

7:118 The son said to him, 'Father, I have sinned against heaven and against you. I am no longer worthy to be called your son.'

7:119 But the father said to his servants, 'Bring the best robe and put it on him. Put a ring on his finger and sandals on his feet.

7:120 Bring the fatted calf and kill it, and let us eat and be merry.

7:121 For this son of mine was dead and is alive again; he was lost and is found.' And they did as they were told and began to be merry.

7:122 Meanwhile, the older son was in the field. As he got close to the house, he heard music and dancing.

7:123 And he called one of the servants and asked what these things meant.

7:124 And the servant answered him saying, 'Your brother has come, and your father has killed the fatted calf because he has him back safe and sound.'

7:125 The older brother became angry and would not go in. So his father came out and pleaded with him.

7:126 But he answered his father, 'Look! All these years I have served you and never disobeyed your orders. Yet you never gave me even a young goat so I could make merry with my friends.

7:127 But as soon as this son comes back, who has devoured what you gave him with harlots, you kill the fatted calf for him!'

7:128 And the father said, 'Son, you are always with me, and everything I have is yours.

7:129 But it is proper that we should make merry and be glad, for this brother of yours was dead and is alive again; he was lost and is found.'"

The Parable of the Lost Coin
Lk 15:8-10

7:130 "Suppose a woman has ten silver coins and loses one. Does she not light a lamp, sweep the house and search diligently until she finds it?

7:131 And when she finds it, she calls her friends and neighbors together and says, 'Rejoice with me; I have found my lost coin.'

7:132 Likewise I say to you, there is joy in the presence of the angels of God over one sinner who repents."

Chapter Eight

THE FINAL EVENTS

Introduction

The pace of the story picks up rapidly as the complicated final events unfold. We already know that the wealthy Roman merchants who owned the vending concessions at the Temple had decided to eliminate Jesus. One of his most trusted disciples, Judas, was threatened by the Romans and forced to betray Jesus. Judas did not believe any real harm would come to Jesus because Judas, like the other disciples, believed that Jesus was indestructible and would lead them into the coming of the Kingdom of Heaven.

Some time after Jesus' arrival in Jerusalem the holiday of Passover began. Passover is an eight day holiday and it is celebrated with a special Passover meal called the Seder. Then, as today, certain customs were practiced during the Seder, including breaking of the Matzoh (unleavened bread) and drinking cups of wine. The history of the exodus of the Israelites from Egypt is retold and special holiday songs are sung. A special meal is prepared. It is a holiday much like the American feast of Thanksgiving, with family and friends sharing the holiday Seder together.

During the Seder, Jesus prophesied that Judas would betray him and, embarrassed, Judas left the group to do just that. After the Seder, Jesus was feeling very melancholy and needed time to himself for reflection and prayer. Shortly thereafter two Roman guards came to arrest Jesus and he was taken away. The disciples, with the exception of Peter, fled for their lives, though as it turned out their lives were not in danger.

However, by following Jesus, Peter's life might have been in danger, but he avoided it by denying that he was one of Jesus' people.

The gospels say the guards took Jesus to the high priest Caiaphas and the Jewish supreme court, called the Sanhedrin, but they were not in session due to the Passover holiday. And its puzzling why the Roman guards would take him to anything Jewish? Rather, they naturally took him to be tried by the Roman government, in this case the Roman governor, Pontius Pilate. Pilate was in cahoots with the Roman merchants and also was warned that Jesus could be a figure to spark unrest and even revolution among the pilgrims. So the fix was in. But being the showman he was, he asked the assembled crowd what they wanted to do with Jesus, and the crowd, composed exclusively of a mob hired by the Roman merchants, called for Jesus' execution.

Jesus was executed in the cruel way typically used by the Romans in those days – the slow death of crucifixion. In his despair Jesus cried out to God and God heard him and comforted him, and then he died. Jesus did not see the coming of the Messiah in his own day, and his followers did not either. In those prophesies Jesus was wrong. But his dedication to the Lord and to his people, the Jews, was rewarded as Jesus was carried off to heaven after his death. The disciples, hearing that his body was no longer in the tomb, had their belief renewed that Jesus was indeed indestructible. They proclaimed that he was the Messiah and said that he would return again to bring the Kingdom of Heaven. The people who believed this became Christians (Christ is Greek for Messiah), and those who did not remained Jews. The rest, as they say, is history.

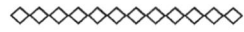

Judas Agrees to Betray Jesus
Mt 26:14-16; Mk 14:10, 11;Lk 22:3-6

8:1 Then the rich merchants whose businesses had been disrupted by Jesus complained about him to the Roman government.

8:2 And they plotted to have Jesus arrested on some charge, for the merchants wanted him dead. The merchants were very powerful and of great influence and were able to make the government do their bidding.

8:3 So they sent out two Roman guards with instructions to bring one of Jesus' followers to them.

8:4 They found one of the Twelve alone—the one called Judas Iscariot—and threatened to kill him unless he helped them capture Jesus.

8:5 Judas did not believe they could hurt Jesus, so he asked "What are you willing to give me if I hand him over to you?" They decided to give him thirty silver coins to do their bidding.

8:6 From then on Judas watched for an opportunity to hand him over.

The Last Supper
Mt 26:17-30; Mk 14:12-26; Lk 22:7-34

8:7 On the first day of the Passover holiday, when it was customary to eat unleavened bread and sacrifice the Paschal lamb as part of the traditional Jewish Seder ceremony, the disciples came to Jesus and asked, "Where do you want us to go to make preparations to celebrate the Passover?"

8:8 So he sent two of his disciples, telling them, "Go into the city, and a man carrying a jar of water will meet you. Follow him.

8:9 And wherever he shall go in, say to the owner of the house, 'The Teacher asks: Where is your guest room, where I may celebrate the Passover Seder with my disciples?'

8:10 He will show you a large upper room, furnished and prepared. There make it ready for us."

8:11 So the disciples did as Jesus had directed them and prepared the Passover Seder.

8:12 When evening came, Jesus was reclining at the table with the Twelve and he interrupted the Seder to say:

8:13 "I tell you the truth, one of you will betray me this very night."

8:14 They were very disturbed and protested to him one after the other, "Surely not I, Master?"

8:15 When Judas, the one who would betray him, said in turn, "Surely not I, Master?" Jesus looked at him sadly and answered, "Yes, I know it is you."

8:16 With everyone looking at him with fury, Judas hastily left the table and the house.

8:17 Then Jesus told them, "This very night you will all leave me, for when the shepherd is struck, the sheep of the flock will be scattered."

8:18 Peter replied, "Even if all fall away on account of you, I never will. I am ready to go with you to prison and death."

8:19 "I tell you the truth," Jesus answered, "this very night, before the rooster crows, you will deny me three times."

8:20 But Peter declared, "Even if I have to die with you, I will never disown you." And all the other disciples said the same.

8:21 Continuing the Seder, Jesus took the unleavened bread, gave thanks and broke it, and gave a piece to each of his disciples, saying,

8:22 "Take and eat; for this is the symbol of the day that the Lord took us out of Egypt to give us our freedom. May we see freedom again in our own day."

8:23 Then they took the first cup of wine, and Jesus raised his cup and said,

8:24 "This is the wine of freedom, that you shall know our freedom will always be sweet." And all drank from their cups.

8:25 When they had finished the Passover Seder, with food and wine and prayers and songs, they went out to the Mount of Olives.

Jesus Arrested

Mt 26:36-56, 69-75; Mk 14:32-50, 66-72; Lk 22:40-62; Jn 18:1-11, 15-18, 25-27

8:26 Then Jesus went with his disciples to a place called Gethsemane on the Mount of Olives, and he said to them, "Sit here while I go over there and pray."

8:27 He took with him Peter and the two sons of Zebedee, and he began to feel sorrowful and heavy.

8:28 Then he said to them, "My soul is exceedingly sorrowful to the point of death. Stay here and keep watch with me."

8:29 And they did so, because they had seen him sad many times before, nearly overcome by the weight of his mission.

8:30 And he went a little farther, and he fell with his face to the ground and prayed, "My Father, I am greatly afraid for what awaits me.

8:31 If it be possible, let this cup pass from me, for I want to live to see the coming of the Kingdom of Heaven. Yet, not as I will, but as You will."

8:32 Then he returned to his disciples and found them sleeping.

8:33 And he said to Peter, "Could you men not keep watch with me for one hour?"

8:34 "Watch and pray so that you will not fall into temptation. The spirit is willing, but the flesh is weak."

8:35 He went away a second time and prayed, "My Father, if it is not possible for this cup to pass away from me unless I drink it, Your will be done.

8:36 But I pray Thee, please protect me from evil so that I may see the coming of the Kingdom of Heaven."

8:37 When he came back, he again found them sleeping, because their eyes were heavy with food and wine.

8:38 So he left them and went away once more and prayed the third time, saying the same thing.

8:39 Then he returned to the disciples and said to them, "It is okay. Sleep on now and rest yourselves.

8:40 For now the hour is at hand, and I see I am already betrayed into the hands of the evil ones. Here comes my betrayer!"

8:41 While he was still speaking, Judas Iscariot returned.

8:42 With him were two officers from the Roman army accompanied by a large mob armed with swords and clubs, hired by the Roman merchants who had plotted against him.

8:43 Now Judas Iscariot had arranged a signal with them: "The one I kiss is the man you are looking for. Then you can arrest him."

8:44 Going at once to Jesus, Judas said, "Forgive me, Master!" and kissed him.

8:45 Jesus replied, "Friends, do what you came for." Then the two officers stepped forward, seized Jesus and arrested him.

8:46 With that, Peter reached for his sword, drew it out and struck one of the officers and cut off his ear.

8:47 "Put your sword back in its place," Jesus said to him, "for all who take the sword will die by the sword. This man is just doing what he has been commanded to do."

The Book of Emet

8:48 And he touched the man's ear and healed him.

8:49 Then Jesus said to the mob that was with the two officers, "Am I like a thief, that you have come with swords and clubs to take me? Every day you saw me teaching in the Temple courts, and you saw the healings I did."

8:50 But the mob became loud and menacing, and all the disciples saw this and deserted him and fled, lest they also be condemned.

8:51 The two officers had been ordered to take Jesus to Pontius Pilate, the governor of Judea.

8:52 Peter followed the guards to see what would happen. He entered the courtyard and sat down with the servants to see the outcome and warmed himself at their fire.

8:53 While Peter was below in the courtyard, one of the servant girls who worked there came by.

8:54 When she saw Peter warming himself by the fire, she looked at him and said "You were also with Jesus of Nazareth."

8:55 But he denied it before them all. "I don't know what you're talking about," he said and moved to the gateway.

8:56 Then the servant girl saw him again and said, "This fellow was with Jesus of Nazareth."

8:57 He denied it again, with an oath: "I don't know the man!"

8:58 After a little while, those standing there went up to Peter and said, "Surely you are one of them, for your Galilean accent gives you away."

8:59 Then he began to call down curses on himself and he swore to them, "I don't know this man you're talking about." Then he heard a rooster crow.

8:60 And Peter remembered the words Jesus had spoken: "Before the rooster crows, you will deny me three times." And he went outside and wept bitterly.

8:61 Now Judas was surprised to hear that Jesus was condemned for he knew Jesus was guiltless and special to God.

8:62 He was seized with a terrible remorse and wanted to return the thirty silver coins to the Roman merchants who had given them to him.

8:63 "I have sinned," he said, "for I have betrayed innocent blood."

8:64 "What is that to us?" they replied. "That is your responsibility."

8:65 So Judas took the coins and threw them into the Temple and left. Then he went away and hanged himself.

Jesus Before Pontius Pilate
Mt 27:11-31; Mk 15:2-20;Lk 23:1-25; Jn 18:29-40

8:66 Jesus was bound by the Roman officers and handed over to Pontius Pilate, the evil and murderous Roman governor of Judea, who had the sole power of life or death in Judea.

8:67 Pilate had financial and social associations with the wealthy and powerful Roman merchants who wanted Jesus dead and had already been bribed by them to order Jesus killed.

8:68 And he remembered the warning Herod had given him about Jesus being called King of the Jews, by virtue of being a descendant from the House of David. And he worried that the people would make a revolt in his name.

8:69 "Are you the King of the Jews as they say?" he asked. "It is you who says it," Jesus replied.

8:70 Then Pilate asked him, "Aren't you going to answer? Don't you hear the testimony they are bringing against you?"

The Book of Emet

8:71 But Jesus made no reply, not even to a single charge.

8:72 Now it was the governor's custom at the time of Jewish Feasts to release a prisoner chosen by the crowd.

8:73 A man called Barabbas was in prison as one of the Jewish insurrectionists who had killed Roman soldiers during an unsuccessful uprising.

8:74 So when the crowd had gathered in the courtyard, Pilate asked them,

8:75 "Which one do you want me to release to you: Barabbas the killer, or Jesus who they say calls himself King of the Jews?"

8:76 The Roman merchants had packed the courtyard with the same hired mob that had helped arrest Jesus. They were instructed to ask for Barabbas instead of Jesus.

8:77 The people who were there to support Jesus saw dozens of armed Roman soldiers surrounding them and they were afraid to try to outshout the mob. Those who did try were quickly beaten and silenced.

8:78 "Which of the two do you want me to release to you?" asked the governor. The mob shouted "We want Barabbas."

8:79 "What shall I do, then, with Jesus who is called King of the Jews?" Pilate asked with great pomposity.

8:80 The mob shouted, "Crucify him!"

8:81 "Why? What crime has he committed?" asked Pilate, continuing the charade.

8:82 And the mob kept shouting "Crucify him! Crucify him!"

8:83 Pilate played along with the mob. He dipped his hands in a cistern of water and washed his hands in front of the crowd.

8:84 "I am innocent of this man's blood," he said. "It is your responsibility!" And the mob cheered wildly.

8:85 Then he released Barabbas to the priests (later to be rearrested after the Feast days were over and quietly executed).

8:86 And he had Jesus flogged publicly, and handed him over to the Roman soldiers to be crucified.

8:87 Then the soldiers took Jesus into the Praetorium and a group of soldiers gathered around him. They plied themselves with wine and decided to have sport with him.

8:88 They stripped him and put a purple robe on him, and then twisted together a crown of thorns and put it on his head.

8:89 They put a staff in his right hand for a scepter and bowed before him and mocked him, saying "Hail, King of the Jews!"

8:90 Then they blindfolded him, spit on him, and took turns striking him on the head again and again with the staff.

8:91 And they mocked him, asking him "Prophesy! Which one of us hit you?" After they were done mocking him, they took off the robe and led him away to be crucified.

The Crucifixion
Mt 27:32-44; Mk 15:21-32;Lk 23:26-43; Jn 19:17-24

8:92 As they were going out, they found a man from Cyrene, named Simon, and they compelled him to carry the cross.

8:93 A large number of people followed him, including his women followers who mourned and wailed for him.

8:94 But Jesus turned to them and said, "Daughters of Jerusalem, do not weep for me; weep for yourselves and for your children.

The Book of Emet

8:95 For the time will come when they will say, 'Blessed are the barren women, the wombs that never bore and the breasts that never nursed!'

8:96 Then they will say to the mountains, 'Fall on us!' and to the hills, 'Cover us!'

8:97 For if men do these things when the tree is green, what will happen when it is dry?"

8:98 They came to a place called Golgotha (called Calvary in Latin). And it was there that the soldiers attached him to the cross.

8:99 Above his head they placed the written accusation against him: THIS IS JESUS, THE KING OF THE JEWS.

8:100 Two thieves were crucified with him, one on his right and one on his left.

8:101 The leaders of the mob passed by and hurled insults at him,

8:102 "Save yourself! If you are the Messiah, come down from the cross!

8:103 "He saved others, but he can't save himself! He's the King of Israel? Let him come down now from the cross, and we will believe him.

8:104 He says he trusts in an invisible God. Let this God rescue him now if He wants him, for his followers say 'He is the Messiah.'"

8:105 The soldiers also came up and mocked him. They offered him wine vinegar; but after tasting it, he refused to drink it.

8:106 One of the thieves who hung there hurled insults at him also: "If you are the Messiah, save yourself and us too!"

8:107 But the other robber rebuked him. "We are being punished for what we did. But this man has done nothing wrong."

8:108 Then he said, "Master, remember me when you go to heaven."

8:109 Jesus answered him, "Today you will surely be with me in paradise."

The Death of Jesus
Mt 27:45-66; Mk 15:33-47; Lk 23:44-56; Jn 19:28-42

8:110 From the sixth hour until the ninth hour darkness came over all the land.

8:111 At the ninth hour Jesus cried out in agony in a loud voice, "Eloi, Eloi, lama sabachthani?"—which means, "My God, my God, why have you forsaken me?"

8:112 When some of those standing there heard this, they said, "He must be calling the prophet Elijah."

8:113 And the leaders of the mob laughed and said, "Let's see if Elijah comes to save him."

8:114 And then Jesus cried out again in a loud voice, and this time God answered him.

8:115 And God said "Be comforted my son, for it is partly through you and your followers that my covenant with Abraham will be fulfilled, that his seed shall be as plentiful as the sands of the seashore and the stars in the sky."

8:116 And Jesus was comforted, and as he felt his life slipping away, he sanctified the name of God (Kiddush HaShem) like the Jewish martyrs of old, by reciting the Shema.

8:117 "Shema Yisrael Adonai Eloheinu Adonai Echad, Hear O Israel, the Lord is our God, the Lord is One."

8:118 Then he fell into a deep sleep and he drew his last breath.

8:119 At that moment the sky grew dark, there was a great storm, and the earth shook.

8:120 When the centurions who were guarding Jesus saw the storm and the earthquake, they were terrified, and exclaimed, "Surely this man was favored by the gods!"

8:121 When all the people who had gathered to witness this sight saw what took place, they beat their breasts and went away.

8:122 But all those who knew him, including the women who had followed him from Galilee, stood at a distance, watching these things. Among them were Mary Magdalene and the mother of Zebedee's two sons.

8:123 As Sabbath Eve approached, there came a rich man from Arimathea, named Joseph, who was also a follower of Jesus.

8:124 And he went to Pontius Pilate and he asked for Jesus' body, and Pilate ordered that it be given to him.

8:125 Joseph took the body, wrapped it in linen, and placed it in a sepulcher that had been hewn out of a rock.

8:126 He rolled a big stone in front of the entrance to the sepulcher and went away.

8:127 Mary Magdalene and the other women mourned in front of the sepulcher.

8:128 The next day, the Roman merchants went to Pilate.

8:129 "Your Excellency," they said, "we are concerned that his disciples may come and steal the body and bury him in a secret place

8:130 and tell the people that here lays the martyr Jesus, the King of the Jews.

8:131 And they will use him to make rebellion against you and us."

8:132 "Take two guards," Pilate answered. "Go, make the tomb as secure as you know how."

8:133 So they went and made the tomb secure by putting a seal on the stone and posting the guards.

The Resurrection
Mt 28:1-20; Mk 16:1-20; Lk 24:1-53; Jn 20:1-31

8:134 On Sunday morning, after the Sabbath day, Mary Magdalene and some of the other women went back to mourn at the tomb.

8:135 But when they arrived there, they saw that the stone, which was very large, had been rolled away.

8:136 As they entered the tomb, they saw an angel dressed in a white robe sitting on the right side of the sepulcher, and they were alarmed.

8:137 His face was like lightning, and his clothes were white as snow. The guards were so afraid of him that they shook and became like dead men.

8:138 The angel said to the women, "Do not be afraid, for I know that you are looking for Jesus of Nazareth, who was crucified.

8:139 He is not here; for the prophet Elijah has come for him and has taken him up on a cloud

8:140 to join with Abraham and Moses and Elijah and sit at the foot of the Lord our God who is in heaven."

8:141 When the disciples were told this by the women, they were encouraged, and they went out among the people

8:142 declaring that Jesus was the Messiah all had been waiting for, and that he would soon come again and save the world.

8:143 And although it did not happen in their lifetimes, as they expected, the disciples of Jesus and their progeny fulfilled God's promise to Abraham,

The Book of Emet

8:144 and they spread the word of the one God throughout the Western world.

8:145 And many years later, we are told, another messenger will rise in the East to also spread the word of the One God.

8:146 And God smiled, for He knew that one day all His children would be reconciled and worship the One God in harmony and peace.

8:147 My name is Emet son of Chaim, and I was Jesus' best friend from the age of three until his death, and I saw or was told about all the things I have written herein.

www.ingramcontent.com/pod-product-compliance
Lightning Source LLC
Chambersburg PA
CBHW071302040426
42444CB00009B/1840